To my wife Daisy Garrido Valdés

I cannot imagine life's journey without your

unconditional love and your timely encouragement!

To Jessica and Juan Elías my heroes,

who along with your mom are my greatest earthly

treasures!

" *I cannot teach anybody anything, I can only make them think.* "

Socrates

" *In the course of scrutiny and kindly testing by men who proceed by question and answer without ill will, with a sudden flash there shines forth understanding about every problem.* "

Plato

" *We live in a world where unfortunately the distinction between true and false appears to become increasingly blurred by manipulation of facts, by exploitation of uncritical minds, and by the pollution of the language.* "

Arne Tiselius

(Nobel Prized–Biochemist)

CRASH COURSE IN CRITICAL THINKING

Table of Contents

FOREWORD

Alex McFarland

Seven centuries before the birth of Christ the prophet Isaiah, writing as directed by God's Holy Spirit, penned the invitation, "Come now, let us reason together" (1:18). The biblical God enjoins the creatures made in His image (that's we humans, by the way) … to think. We are to reason, and we are to do it well. God is glorified when people think well and behave reasonably. Christianity is unique among belief systems regarding the premium it places on rational thought. I realize that this statement would come as a surprise to many moderns whose image of Christianity is really but a caricature.

Because God is a rational, logical, and orderly God, the universe is an intelligible, comprehensible place. It is possible to discover things that are really true. Actual truth may be discovered, reality can be understood, and real knowledge may be attained. Glory to God!

In addition to the Isaiah passage mentioned, other Scriptures (such as Proverbs 1-3) urge people to think correctly, seek truth, and look to God for wisdom. In programming the hearts of people to "seek truth," our Creator has extended to humans the holy calling (it is a mandate, really) to think logically. God has even given as a toolkit to help in this endeavor, a resource carried within each of us, the laws (or principles) of logic. In this fine book, penned by one of the most godly and wise men I have ever had the privilege to know, you will learn to identify and use the basic principles of logic.

Some say that logic is a human invention. False. Many well-known thinkers have pursued the rules of reason, written about them, and have categorized examples of right and wrong thinking (these would include Socrates, Solomon, Aquinas, C. S. Lewis, to name a few). Man has discovered reason, but he didn't invent rationality. This is a rational universe and we can think within the bounds of logic because God (the Creator and foundation of all reality) is a reasonable Being. It is altogether appropriate to offer our minds for the service of God, and to ask Him to make them the best they may be (see James 1:5).

Millions today have been raised /conditioned to think illogically if not reject the idea of truth outright. Most of these people- groping through life amidst a haze of relativism- are not even aware that "denial of truth" has become their default perspective. In composing this "Christian tutorial on better thinking," my dear friend, Juan Valdes is serving the needs of many people. Juan is himself a meticulous thinker and a brilliant Christian scholar.

I commend his scholarship to readers everywhere. I believe that the Lord will use Juan's book to equip many for the exposure of that which is false and toward the apprehension of that which is good, true, and beautiful.

Alex McFarland

October, 2014

HOW
TO
USE

THIS BOOK

This book is written to be used as a text book for learning basic skills and principles of critical thinking. It will require hard work, but it can be very rewarding. I recommend that the book be studied chapter by chapter in the order presented and each chapter should be mastered prior to proceeding to the next. The content of each chapter builds a foundation for the following chapter. This is particularly true beginning with chapter 4. The Introduction and chapters 1-3 are free standing and very practical for engaging in critical thinking about ideas in general. In chapters 4-7, I cover the critical components of argumentation, and these should be studied in order prior to engaging with the fallacies. The toughest chapter in the book is chapter 8, and is optional. It is recommended for students who are strong logical thinkers because it requires higher order thinking skills and a thorough knowledge of materials covered in chapters 4-6. Finally, chapters 9-10 present, arguably, the most useful section of the book and can be studied independently of the rest of the book or in conjunction with the previous chapters. At the end of the book there is an appendix with exercises for each chapter. These exercises include Key Terms followed by application and higher order thinking exercises that begin mild in Think About It and progress to much more challenging exercises in Think A Little Harder.

Some chapters also include Skill Drills, which offer the student practice exercises to apply specific skills learned in the chapter. The last part of the exercises is the most challenging, thus the title For the Geniuses. The parent/tutor of the subject can pick and choose what exercises to assign for each chapter. I recommend that the Geniuses questions be optional or extra-credit for most students, unless the student is especially adept at higher order thinking.

In Christ,

Juan Valdes

INTRODUCTION
CRITICAL THINKING

Some people would rather die than have to think. These are the vulnerable masses in society led down every which way by those who do think. Sometimes they are led down the right paths, but more often they are misled. There are countless people in our world who will embrace anything without questioning it as long as the presenter seems believable or they have a vested interest in accepting it. Their response to the ludicrous affirmation that the sky is purple is one of astonishment and embarrassment for not having noticed it sooner. They will continue to believe this until someone posits that the sky is actually green at which point they will blush at their naivety for having believed it was purple, and they will join the green sky club with militant resolve. Sadly, this has led to very tragic consequences both individually and corporately, and Christians are not exempt.

The dangers of not thinking critically are manifest in the annals of history, particularly when we consider the tragic consequences suffered by the mindless masses. History has shown us that many people have been misled, to their own detriment, by the dangerous ideologies of men such as Karl Marx, Adolph Hitler, Fidel Castro, and countless others. Careful consideration of these cases also reveals that lack of critical thinking not only misleads a people into embracing the lies, but it also enslaves them to these ideologies even when their existential reality contradicts the very core of their beliefs. Why are the most militant advocates of the wonders of communism the very people who have witnessed the prosperity of their leaders at the expense of their own hunger? While there are many other factors involved, lack of critical thinking is at the core of the matter.

The Apostle Paul was an ardent advocate of critical thinking. His constant references to the mind and the need to use it and renew it are evidence of the abundance of ignorance that characterized the early church. This is the idea behind Paul's warning to the Christians at Colossae.

Their vulnerability appeared to be driven by a lack of critical thinking. Paul feared they would be "spoiled" by empty and deceptive ideas based on human traditions. His exhortation to the Colossians was that they "Beware" not to be enslaved. The Greek verb *blepo* is used as an imperative that means "beware!" or "look out!" Apparently there were those among the church at Colossae who were not thinking critically.

> *Beware lest any man spoil you through philosophy and vain deceit, after the tradition of men, after the rudiments of the world, and not after Christ (Colossians 2:8, KJV).*

If the ideas were indeed hollow and deceptive, a critical consideration would have uncovered the truth.

Paul makes a similar exhortation to the church at Ephesus where he emphasizes the importance of being taught to think critically.

When we consider the words of verse 14 in particular, what stands out is the fact that many Christians appeared to be vulnerable to any and all teachings. The expressions "tossed to and fro" and "carried about" speak of a total lack of critical thinking skills among these early Christians. What made these Christians so vulnerable? The key lies in that they heard the Gospel of Jesus Christ and embraced it in the same manner as they embraced any other idea. It seems as if they were not thinking even as it relates to the Gospel. Thus, the Gospel was their conviction until someone

> *11 And he gave some, apostles; and some, prophets; and some, evangelists; and some pastors and teachers; 12 For the perfecting of the saints, for the work of the ministry, for the edifying of the body of Christ: 13 Till we all come in the unity of the faith, and of the knowledge of the Son of God, unto a perfect man, unto the measure of the stature of the fullness of Christ: 14 That we henceforth be no more children, tossed to and fro, and carried about with every wind of doctrine, by the sleight of men, and cunning craftiness, whereby they lie in wait to deceive (Ephesians 4:11-14, KJV).*

else came along with a different idea. Therefore, Paul's emphasis here and throughout his letters was on the teaching and discipling of believers. Christians needed to think critically of the Gospel and develop a strong intellectual foundation for what they believed. What about today's church? Are we as Christians any stronger in our convictions? The David

Koreshes and Jim Joneses of modern times show that there continues to be a desperate need for critical thinking.

But what is critical thinking? Let us not be confused by the word "critical." While this word is often associated with being negatively judgmental and fault-finding, that is not the only sense of the word. Critical thinking is about using all of our faculties to evaluate ideas in an attempt to discover their veracity or falsity. Here is an excellent and thorough definition of critical thinking:

> "...critical thinking is the general term given to a wide range of cognitive skills and intellectual dispositions needed to effectively identify, analyze, and evaluate arguments and truth claims; to discover and overcome personal prejudices and biases; to formulate and present convincing reasons in support of conclusions; and to make reasonable, intelligent decisions about what to believe and what to do." [1]

This definition covers the numerous dimensions of critical thinking. Specifically, notice that the definition addresses four dimensions of critical thinking:[2]

1. THE SKILLS REQUIRED TO EVALUATE ARGUMENTS AND TRUTH CLAIMS

This is the primary purpose for this book. As Christians we are constantly being bombarded with dangerous and often antagonistic truth claims, and we need to be able to identify, analyze, and evaluate these claims, prior to accepting them as true. Atheist professors constantly bombard students with truth claims that are hostile to God, Christ, the Bible, etc. Non-Christian friends and family often attempt to persuade us to abandon our faith in response to their arguments. Newspaper articles, magazines, websites, and blogs are constantly striving to persuade us with truth claims that may or may not be true. We need to be able to break these arguments down and evaluate them objectively in order to embrace only those claims which we find to be true.

2. THE SKILLS REQUIRED TO OVERCOME PERSONAL PREJUDICES AND BIASES

A secondary benefit of learning the basics of critical thinking is the ability to identify our own prejudices and biases as they affect our ability to evaluate truth claims. There are a number of ways in which these biases manifest themselves. Sometimes we really want something to be true because it would benefit us greatly. Other times we may be so inclined to believe the person or organization making a claim that the claim itself isn't given due consideration. On other occasions we may fear the consequences of rejecting a truth claim. Whatever the prejudices and biases may be, they keep us from being objective in our evaluations of truth claims.

3. THE SKILLS REQUIRED TO FORMULATE GOOD ARGUMENTS

Equally important to evaluating truth claims presented by others is our ability to present truth claims of our own in a proper format. We need to be able to communicate the Truth of God's Word in valid, sound, and coherent arguments. Our truth claims need to be able to survive the critical analyses of others. Some people will still reject our truth claims, even when these are presented in perfectly good arguments, but their rejection won't stem from objective analysis. Instead, the rejection will often stem from subjective positions, unreasonable stances, or arbitrary choices. If perfect arguments persuaded all who heard them, then Jesus would have been far more successful in his earthly ministry. However, we know that many rejected his truth claims. Those who rejected him had no reasonable or rational basis for their rejection — for his arguments were perfect.

4. THE SKILLS REQUIRED TO MAKE INTELLIGENT DECISIONS ABOUT WHAT TO BELIEVE AND WHAT TO DO

Our lives are full of choices. We make hundreds of choices every day. We know that many of these choices are inconsequential, but there are quite a few that bear an enormous potential for consequences — good or bad. Critical thinking skills provide us with the tools we need to evaluate alternatives and to make better choices. It doesn't mean all of our choices will be perfect, since we often find ourselves having to make decisions without access to all of the information we need to do so intelligently. Nevertheless, even in those situations, we can minimize the potential for bad consequences and maximize the potential for good ones. So let us embark upon the journey to master the basic skills of Critical Thinking.

CHAPTER 1

THE PURSUIT OF TRUTH

We live in a world where people seem to be out of touch with reality. Whether it's due to unrealistic dreams and expectations, misinformation, ignorance, spiritual blindness, or any number of other causes, Truth seems to elude many. Some people go as far as denying the very existence of Truth as an objective reality, adopting instead a relativistic position on truth. In other words, there is no "Truth" with a capital "T." Instead, truth is subjective.

Everyone has his own "truth" which, interestingly, does not have to coincide with anyone else's version of truth. This, of course, is ludicrous and utterly untenable. Therefore, the need for critical thinking is urgent. Why? Because the ultimate goal of critical thinking is finding Truth.

TWO KINDS OF TRUTHS

What do we mean by the word "truth"? Truth is a property of propositions that correspond to the way things are.[1] This is often called the "Correspondence Theory of Truth." Consider the following statement: the Miami Heat defeated the San Antonio Spurs 95-88 in game 7 of the NBA Championship held in Miami on June 20, 2013 to win the National Championship. That statement is absolutely true. Its truthfulness is not dependent on the observer or on anyone's opinion. This is what we call objective truth. A statement is considered objectively true if the truthfulness of it is dependent on the "object" itself and not the "subject" (the observer). In other words, there are truths that are absolutely true, regardless of anyone's' opinion, perception, or understanding.

Consider these statements:

1. 2 + 2 = 4.
2. The Earth revolves around the Sun.
3. Water is composed of one molecule of oxygen and two molecules of hydrogen.
4. On July 21, 1969 Neil Armstrong was the first astronaut to walk on the surface of the moon.
5. God exists.
6. The Bible is God's Word.

Each of these statements is objectively true. While most people don't have a problem with the first four statements, there is much controversy today about statements 5 and 6. However, the truthfulness of these statements is not dependent on anyone's opinion. Either God exists or he does not, and our opinion is irrelevant in shaping the reality of it. Either the Bible is or is not God's Word, and our opinion is irrelevant with regards to the reality of it[2]. These are the types of statements that lead to productive discussions.

Now consider the following statement: "Basketball is the most entertaining sport of all time." This statement is clearly not objectively true. The truthfulness of this statement is dependent on the "subject" or observer; it is a matter of opinion. Some people find another sport to be more entertaining, some find basketball boring, and others don't find sports to be entertaining at all. This is what we call subjective truth. **Consider the following statements:**

1. *Dulce de Leche ice cream is the best ice cream ever.*
2. *69° F. is the perfect temperature to set the air conditioner at night.*
3. *Women look better with long hair.*
4. *Being a doctor is the most rewarding career.*
5. *Atheism is intellectually fulfilling.*
6. *Going to church is boring.*

Each of these statements is subjectively true for the person affirming them. Notice that as a Christian you probably don't agree with statements 5 and 6, but they are a matter of opinion. Thus, when we claim that Atheism is NOT intellectually fulfilling, that is subjectively true for us, but others may not agree. Likewise, when we claim that going to church is awesome, that is subjectively true for us, but others may not agree. Truth in this sense is dependent on the opinion of the subject instead of the object itself. Thus, arguing about subjective truths is usually fruitless.

Our focus should be the pursuit of objective truth. Engaging someone regarding to claim 5 would require a shift into the realm of objectivity. Instead of arguing about intellectual fulfillment, the focus could be changed to whether atheism is true or not. That would be a far more productive discussion.

TESTS OF TRUTH

The importance of establishing the truthfulness of an objective claim cannot be overstated. As we mentioned above, the statement "God exists" is either true or not regardless of our opinion. So how do we determine whether it is true or not? As with any truth claim, there are a number of tests that can be applied to a truth claim to ascertain the veracity of it. However, it is important to distinguish between the nature of truth (correspondence) and various tests that might be necessary to help us recognize truth.[3]

Ronald Nash presents three distinct tests that can go a long way in helping the critical thinker evaluate the veracity of a truth claim: the Test of Correspondence, the Test of Coherence, and the Test of Pragmatism.[4] Let us take a closer look at each of these.

Objective:
Ice cream is a food.

Subjective:
Ice cream is amazing!

TEST OF CORRESPONDENCE

The Test of Correspondence is applied to truth claims by attempting to physically verify the claim. How would one test the claim that my office is 1.5 miles from my home? That would be rather simple: get in a car, reset the mileage trip counter to zero, and drive from my home to my office. If it is indeed 1.5 miles, then my claim would correspond with reality. That simple test would establish whether the claim is true or not. How can we test the truthfulness of someone's claim that God miraculously healed them from a cancerous tumor? Again, the Test of Correspondence would be very effective. A visit to the doctor and a second MRI followed by a comparison of MRI's would show if the tumor has disappeared or not. This test can be very effective in many of the claims made against the Bible, against Christians or Christianity, claims of a scientific nature, etc., but there are claims where the test of correspondence is not available.

TEST OF COHERENCE

In cases where the Test of Correspondence is not applicable, alternative tests are available. The Test of Coherence is one such test in which a proposition's truth is evaluated in terms of how well it coheres with all other relevant information available to us.[5]

> A couple rents a vacation villa in the Florida Keys. In addition, the husband rents a fishing boat for the week. Early every morning he goes fishing and is back at the dock by noon. However on the fourth day of fishing he fails to return home. When he is not back by 5pm, his wife calls the authorities and informs them that something must have happened to her husband. The Coast Guard is notified and within a couple of hours they have located the boat, but no sign of her husband. The boat is found anchored 2 miles off shore and inside they find his shoes, his wallet with several hundred dollars in cash in addition to all of his credit cards, his phone and his expensive Swiss Watch. The Coast Guard continues the search, but a body is never found. Eventually, the wife must call the insurance company to make a claim. That presents a problem for the insurance company.

At this point, how does the insurance company verify the truthfulness of the claim that her husband is dead? Without the body, the test of correspondence is not possible. Hence, all of the evidence is analyzed in order to determine if it all fits together (coheres). After all, it could be a trick to collect his life insurance. But upon closer examination, alternative explanations are ruled out. It wasn't a robbery because all of the valuables were left behind. Everything seems to point to the fact that her husband either fell from the boat and drowned or he went for a swim and drowned.

The Test of Coherence, however, has a few weaknesses. First, it cannot provide physical evidence that proves the correspondence of the claim. Thus its conclusions are at best "highly probable" but not certain. There could be other scenarios where the husband is still alive. Maybe he had someone pick him up in another boat so he can stage a disappearance. Maybe he swam to shore and is disoriented and hasn't found his way home. In addition, this test seems to equate the "completeness" of the information with truth. This test is often used in the United States legal system. A jury is often asked to examine all of the evidence to see if it coheres, beyond reasonable doubt (not beyond all doubt) in order to establish the guilt or innocence of the accused.

TEST OF PRAGMATISM

The Test of Pragmatism is yet another test that can be used to seek the veracity of a particular claim. This test bases the "truthfulness" of a claim on whether it works or not. A good example of this test in action is its application to the claim, "Everyone decides for himself what is right and wrong." Usually, this proposition is followed by its logical conclusion—"Who are we to judge them?" This common proposition of moral relativism is hard to test with correspondence and coherence. However, the Test of Pragmatism does the job beautifully. Does this proposition work? Here, by "work" we mean—is it livable? Can people live out this proposition in everyday life? If everyone decides for himself what is right and wrong, than how can we possibly incarcerate anyone? If a thief decides for himself that stealing is the "right" thing to do, than how can we justify putting him in jail? After all, what he was doing is "right" to him. What if I decide that killing you is "right?" I'm sure that even the staunchest relativist knows that stealing, murder, and rape (among other things) are wrong regardless of what anyone decides. If a person tries to live by this proposition, he would have to be okay with others stealing from him, hurting his loved ones, etc. Nobody lives like that! Thus, the proposition fails the Test of Pragmatism.

Of the three tests, this is probably the weakest. Its biggest problem is that true propositions sometimes appear not to "work" while false propositions sometimes appear to work. An example that is often cited is conflict between the Ptolemaic Model of the Universe and the Copernican Model. Today we all know that the Copernican Model of the Universe, which places the Sun at the center of our solar system and the planets rotating around it, is true. However, when it was first suggested, the Ptolemaic Model, which placed the Earth at the center of our solar system, seemed to work better with the data that was observed, whereas the Copernican Model provided data that didn't work. In other words, the erroneous Ptolemaic Model worked better at explaining the observed data than the Copernican Model, which was correct. It took some time for scientists to figure out why the Copernican Model didn't work, even though they really believed it was correct. As it turned out, Copernicus' model originally had the planets orbiting the Sun in a circular orbit. When that was changed to an elliptical orbit, it worked perfectly, far better than the Ptolemaic Model.

A WORD ON RELATIVISM

The main problem with relativism, in all its forms, is that it applies what we know to be the case regarding subjective truth—truth as a matter of opinion—to objective truth claims. Today's culture wants to put Christianity, God's existence, the reliability of the Bible, the claims of Jesus, etc. under the category of opinion. Sometimes this is due to confusion regarding categories of truth. However, more often, it results from the outright denial of objective truth, when these are obviously objective claims that are true or false independent of anyone's opinion.

> **Today's culture wants to put Christianity, God's existence, the reliability of the Bible, the claims of Jesus, etc. under the category of opinion**

THE BIBLE TEACHES THAT TRUTH IS WORTH PURSUING!

Let us focus on just two amazing passages where the Bible addresses the concept of "truth."[6] Consider the words of Jesus to the disciples in John 8:32, "And ye shall know the truth, and the truth shall make you free." From this we can pick up two foundational concepts regarding truth. First, truth is knowable. Jesus' words leave no room for denying the accessibility of truth. God made us in His image and gave us a mind to be able to acquire knowledge and find truth. Needless to say, the same ability allows us to differentiate between what is true and what is false. Second, our freedom is directly related to our knowledge of truth. Within the context of John 8, it is clear that Jesus is speaking of the deception that Satan uses as his most powerful tool (John 8:44).

This concept has never been more relevant than in today's world where the enemy has embedded his lies deeply in the conscious of the different cultures. The only way to free ourselves from these lies is to know the truth. An alcoholic or drug addict easily buys into the lie that they will always be an addict and that they can never change. If they fail to learn the truth, this becomes a self-fulfilling prophecy. When people don't know the truth, they don't know any better and are stuck in the bondage of sin and death—right where Satan wants them. But upon learning that they can do ALL things through Christ who strengthens them and they learn that Christ died to set them free, they are able to break those chains of addictions. That is why Jesus' words are so powerful—learning the truth gives you access to the power of God and the forgiveness of Jesus.

> **That is why Jesus' words are so powerful–learning the truth gives you access to the power of God and the forgiveness of Jesus.**

Let us then consider Jesus' words to his disciples in John 14:6, "I am the way, the truth, and the life: no man cometh unto the Father, but by me." The enemy knows that if we follow other "truths" we will miss "the Truth" along with all of its benefits—we will miss the way, we will miss the life, and we will not be able to go to the Father. This passage, as well as the previous one, highlights the importance of pursuing TRUTH![7] While this passage contains numerous profound teachings, let us focus on "the truth." Jesus identifies himself as the truth. Thus, the pursuit of truth begins with and ends with truth HIMSELF—Jesus. The way this passage is written in the Greek leaves no room for alternative truths. The article that precedes the word "truth" points to the exclusivity of truth. There is only one source of truth, JESUS! Jesus is the visible incarnation of truth! His teachings are pure truth. Is it any wonder that Satan wishes to attack Truth, the Bible (as God's truth revealed) and the person of Jesus Christ (truth incarnate)?

The following chapters are meant to provide the reader with powerful tools that will aid him in finding truth and correctly distinguishing between what is true and what is false. These tools are meant to tap into the powerful mind God has given us and use it to find Jesus—Truth incarnate. Furthermore, it will equip the reader with very effective tools to communicate the truth to a world enslaved by the lies of the enemy. Let us be bold!

The enemy knows that if we follow other "truths," we will miss "the Truth" along with all of its benefits–we will miss the way, we will miss the life, and we will not be able to go to the Father.

...the pursuit of truth begins
with and ends with truth
HIMSELF—Jesus.

CHAPTER 2

CRITICAL THINKING PRINCIPLES

2

Critical Thinking

There are many key principles that govern critical thinking. As we consider some of these principles you'll notice that each represents a common sense issue that is often neglected. Let us consider six indispensable principles.

SEEK CLARITY!

Say what? You cannot evaluate an idea or an argument if you don't have a clear understanding of exactly what is being said. Debates often linger and remain unresolved because the parties involved are misunderstanding the position presented. Consider the following dialogue that illustrates the importance of clarity in discourse:

Have you ever heard about the song that never ends?

Phil: *"How can you take faith over science?"*

Joe: *"That's easy, because without faith we cannot please God."*

Phil: *"That's why I can never be a Christian, science makes too much sense."*

Joe: *"But God makes sense too! Don't you get it?"*

This is the type of argument that never ends. This argument will go on forever because it lacks clarity. Joe's initial response should have been to seek clarification on what Phil means by "faith." In doing so he would have noticed that they were both using the word faith but were talking about totally different things. Thus, they would never be able to resolve the conflict much to the detriment of Phil's eternal destiny. Phil's definition of faith is provided by our secular culture as "believing in something even when there is a mountain of evidence to the contrary." Joe's definition is all about trusting God, based on His promises and truth (evidence). There really is no conflict between faith and science. The discussion should have been steered towards the compatibility of science and the Bible.

This principle is of utmost importance because people often fail to express themselves clearly. Sometimes we know what we want to say but have a hard time verbalizing it. Other times it is our thoughts that are obscure. This is painfully obvious when one encounters the writings of someone who is struggling to explain difficult ideas. Take the following example from the opening paragraph of Kierkegaard's *The Sickness Unto Death,*

> A human being is spirit. But what is spirit? Spirit is the self. But what is the self? The self is a relation that relates itself to itself or is the relation's relating itself to itself in the relation; the self is not the relation but is the relation's relating itself to itself. A human being is a synthesis of the infinite and the finite, of the temporal and the eternal, of freedom and necessity, in short, a synthesis. A synthesis is a relation between two. Considered in this way, a human being is still not a self.
>
> In the relation between the two, the relation is the third as a negative unity, and the two relate to the relation and in the relation to the relation; thus under the qualification of the psychical the relation between the psychical and the physical is a relation. If, however, the relation relates itself to itself, this relation is the positive third, and this is the self.[1]

HUH?? What if you were asked the simple question, "Do you agree with him or not?" How would you go about answering the question? While it may be very profound, it is impossible for us to evaluate his position without seeking clarity. There are some key questions we need to get in the habit of asking before we even begin to evaluate an idea.

> *Could you elaborate further?*
>
> *Could you give me an example?*
>
> *Could you illustrate what you mean?*
>
> *What do you mean by the word _____?*

As critical thinkers we need to work diligently for clarity of both thoughts and language.

STRIVE FOR ACCURACY!

Almost accurate is not good enough. Having inaccurate information usually leads to faulty conclusions. It is very common for people to rattle-off unverified or erroneous information as if it were undisputable fact. Whether it is done purposely or not, the effect on the discussion is the same. A critical thinker always questions the accuracy of the "facts" that are presented in a discussion. The following dialogue illustrates the importance of accuracy in discourse.

> **Car Salesman:** *"This Chevy Suburban is very fuel efficient!"*
>
> **Naïve buyer:** *"Great! That's exactly what I'm looking for. I need to save money on gas."*

What is the obvious question that a critical thinker would be making? How fuel efficient is the Chevy Suburban? It seems obvious that a critical thinker will question the accuracy of the claim that such a large vehicle is very fuel efficient.

In order for the buyer to make an intelligent decision, he needs to be given accurate data. Inaccuracies also make their way into print. The internet is completely inundated with articles, studies, and discussions that are completely inaccurate. Many people seem to miss the fact that anybody can put up a website, a blog, or a video without having to verify that the content is accurate. Numerous emails circulate with stories that are confirmed urban legends, and yet people believe them and pass them on as if they were factual. Consider some of the following inaccurate statements and stories circulated online.

ONLINE INACCURACIES

1. Scientists drilling in Northern Russian find hell several miles under the surface of the earth. Click here to listen to the recordings of the people screaming.
2. Microsoft donates $1.00 for every person you forward this email to.
3. We only use 10% of our brain.
4. Elvis is still alive and was seen as recently as last week in Las Vegas.
5. The rock band's name KISS is an acronym for Knights (or Kings) in Satan's Service.

Every one of these statements is patently false and inaccurate, and yet you can find them either online or in emails all over the internet presented as absolute fact. A critical thinker must inquire and verify the accuracy of what he reads online prior to making any type of evaluation or decision on an issue.

PURSUE PRECISION!

Lack of precision has been very instrumental in the process of misdirecting and deceiving naïve and unsuspecting people. There are an abundance of purposely imprecise words that find their way strategically into arguments. Words such as **many, most, a lot,** almost everybody, and the majority should raise red flags in the mind of a critical thinker. How much is many? How much is a lot? It is quite common for someone to appeal to these vague terms in order to "prove" the acceptance or accuracy of the idea or position being posited.

Further, these vague words seem to imply that those who disagree are in the minority. Consider the following argument: What would the response of a critical thinker be to Robbie's statement?

> Robbie: *"Most scientists agree that the theory of multiverses provides the best explanation for the precision of the physical constants in our universe that make it perfectly balanced for human life."*
>
> Joe: *"Well, if most scientists agree than I guess I am wrong."*

In pursuing precision, some good questions would include: Could you be more precise about the number of scientists who affirm the multiverse theory? What study or survey did you get the information from? What was the margin of error in the survey? How many scientists did not agree with the theory of multiverses? Who are some of the scientists that would disagree with the theory of multiverses? All of these questions seek more precision. Both 51% and 96% can be said to represent "most" in any given argument, but it is obvious that the implications of each are quite different.[2] Lack of precision is usually the sign of a weak argument.

DEMAND CONSISTENCY!

Inconsistency is an ice cream that comes in two distinct flavors. Inconsistencies come in both the practical and the logical flavors. These are very common in everyday discourse. **Consider the following two scenarios.**

SCENARIO 1: Professor Smith introduced himself to his freshman biology students affirming that something can only be accepted as "truth" if it can be proven scientifically.

SCENARIO 2: In a college writing class the professor advises the class as follows: "Always use simple language. Adjure sesquipedalian parlance and recrementitious argot. Never use bombastic and magniloquent balderdash."

These two scenarios highlight two common types of inconsistency. In Scenario 1 there is a direct contradiction (inconsistency) between two beliefs being held by the professor. His claim does not meet his own criteria for truth. His claim that *"something can only be accepted as truth if it can be proven scientifically"* cannot be proven *scientifically.* This is known as a logical inconsistency, its self-defeating. which involves saying or believing inconsistent things. Critical thinkers need to listen carefully for the logical inconsistencies present in many arguments and truth claims. In one conversation, a moral relativist will insist that everyone chooses for themselves what is right and what is wrong and we are nobody to judge them. Then in another conversation the moral relativist will be upset because someone stole his car and believes that person was wrong to do so and should be punished. Do you see the logical inconsistency? If everyone has the right to decide what is right and wrong for themselves and we cannot judge them for it, then why are we judging the car thief and accusing him of having done something wrong?

In Scenario 2 we have a contradiction between what is said and what is done. This is known as a practical inconsistency which involves saying one thing and doing another. Inconsistency of either type is a "red flag" that should make us wary. A very common example shows up when someone is attempting to promote moral relativism. It is common for someone to attack a Christian as intolerant by expressing something like, "It is wrong for you to be telling people they are wrong. Everyone has a right to do as they please!" Do you see the logical inconsistency? The person is presenting a truth claim that it is wrong to tell someone they are wrong and everyone has a right to do what they please, but the person is violating her own truth claims by telling the Christian he is wrong and he doesn't have a right to do what he pleases. This shows an obvious inconsistency between what is said and what is done. If we don't listen carefully, we may not even notice the inconsistency.

INSIST THAT ARGUMENTS MAKE LOGICAL SENSE!

Some arguments sound great, but unfortunately they are illogical. A common mistake is to draw conclusions that don't necessarily follow from the argument presented. In the field of logic, this is a well-known fallacy called non-sequitur.[3] In order to properly evaluate these statements, we need to separate the facts from the conclusions drawn from those facts. If the conclusions don't necessarily follow, then the argument is illogical. Consider the following examples.

> **EXAMPLE 1:** Johnny got an "F" on the math assignment. He must not have studied very much.

THE FACT: Johnny got an "F" on the math assignment.
THE CONCLUSION: He must not have studied very much.
PROBLEM: There are many other reasons why Johnny may have gotten an "F." He may have studied and then forgotten the material. There may be an error in the teacher's answer key. The questions on the test may not have been covered in the material that was to be studied, etc.

> **EXAMPLE 2:** *My kitchen burned down and it's your fault! If you had not called me, I would not have answered the phone, and thus I would not have forgotten about the pot on the stove, and thus the pot would never have caught fire. Don't call me again!*

THE FACT: The kitchen burned down.

THE CONCLUSION: If you had not called the kitchen would not have burned down.

PROBLEM: The fire in the kitchen was not caused by the phone call. Furthermore, the person could have taken the call and kept an eye on the stove. Or the kitchen could have burned down anyway had another distraction kept you from watching the pot, etc.

> **EXAMPLE 3:** *Mr. Gribendorf is the best teacher in the school because he lets us "chill" and gives us all 100's on our tests.*

THE FACT: Mr. Gribendorf allows students to "chill," and he gives all of his students 100s on their tests.

THE CONCLUSION: He is the best teacher in the school.

PROBLEM: How Mr. Gribendorf grades tests does not make him the best teacher. There are many other factors involved. The amount of "chill" time given by Mr. Gribendorf does not make him the best teacher. Furthermore, clarification should be demanded regarding the definition of the word best. The best teacher from a parent's perspective may be quite different than the best teacher from a student's perspective.

KEEP THE DISCOURSE RELEVANT!

"Baloney" detection is an art. When we engage in a discussion or debate, detecting baloney becomes a powerful tool. One of the most difficult skills in critical thinking is being able to stay focused enough on the issue being discussed to detect when someone is trying to introduce irrelevant issues (baloney) as a distraction. In logic this is known as introducing a red herring. Our tendency is to engage the irrelevant issue and attempt to respond to it, when we should be dismissing it as irrelevant. It is important to keep in mind that the irrelevant issue may or may not be true, but it has nothing to do with the issue at hand.

Consider the following examples:

> **EXAMPLE 1:** *"I think abortion should be allowed! Look at how many hungry and starving children are out there already, we don't need any more suffering children!"*

If the topic at hand is the legalization of abortion, than arguments have to be presented that are relevant. A critical thinker will not let himself be drawn into discussions of world hunger and suffering amongst children because these topics are irrelevant.

EXAMPLE 2: *"The drinking age should be lowered to 18! How can you be old enough to join the military and not old enough to drink?"*

If the point is to argue that the drinking age should be lowered to 18, than arguments have to be presented that explain why 18 is better than 21. A critical thinker will not let himself be drawn into a discussion of the legal age to join the military because that is completely irrelevant.

EXAMPLE 3: *"Smoking marijuana should be legal! There are many people who enjoy it!"*

The number of people who enjoy smoking marijuana is irrelevant in the discussion of legalizing the smoking of marijuana. That's the same as arguing that stealing should be legal and basing the argument on the fact that many people enjoy stealing. The fact that people enjoy something is not relevant to the legality of it.

EXAMPLE 4 : *"Carla should not marry Peter! Statistics show that 73% of marriages end in divorce."*

Relevant arguments would have to deal with specific reasons why the marriage of these two would not be a good idea. Divorce statistics are irrelevant in proving the point that Carla should not marry Peter. In each of these examples, the main issue is put aside when an irrelevant issue is introduced. If the person who responds to these arguments fails to see them for what they are and falls for the diversion, the main issue is abandoned and the presenter has successfully changed the subject. Each of the six principles of critical thinking is of utmost importance in keeping the critical thinker from falling into the traps of bad arguments. Whether an argument is being analyzed or one is being developed, it is always wise to apply the principles as part of the process.

OBSTACLES TO CRITICAL THINKING

3

STOP
NO CRITICAL THINKING BEYOND THIS POINT

People usually think they are right. When people engage in evaluating ideas, it is often difficult for them to be critical of their own views. Nicholas Rescher gives us a useful list of six obstacles that have the tendency to impede critical thinking.[1]

CRITICAL THINKING ROADBLOCKS!

1. Prejudices and "passions": hatred, fear, envy, greed, etc.

2. Conformity: just "going with the flow" to do the popularly done thing rather than thinking things through.

3. Personal Commitment: affinity, loyalty, and affective involvement with particular individuals and cliques.

4. Ideological or political allegiances.

5. Personal bias: giving credit or discredit by appreciation or "symbolic" connection rather than on merit.

6. "Wishful thinking"; being guided by our own desires and conveniences rather than by evidence and argument.

Let's consider these as we find them in everyday life.

PREJUDICES AND "PASSIONS": HATRED, FEAR, ENVY, GREED, ETC.

Emotions have a way of clouding our judgment! We often find ourselves reacting to ideas without thinking critically because either the idea, the source of the idea, or the way the idea was presented provokes an emotional response. As a Christian apologist, I have to struggle with this personally. It is not easy to listen to someone attack me personally instead of engaging with my truth claims. My first reaction is a strong desire to retaliate, but the Word of God is clear that we are to engage with the lost with an attitude of "meekness and fear" (1 Peter 3:15). In other words, we must have an attitude of gentleness and respect towards those with whom we engage. Sometimes the attack is against my faith, and that is equally difficult to deal with. Honestly, it angers me tremendously when someone seems to have no respect for God, Jesus, or the Word. However, we cannot lose our objectivity. We need to take a step back from the emotional reaction and think critically about both the arguments being thrown at us and the arguments we use in response.

Anger is not the only emotion that clouds our judgment. Fear is another formidable obstacle to critical thinking. Sometimes we are gripped by fear of failure, fear of judgment, fear of embarrassment, as well as other common fears, and this keeps us from engaging critically with the ideas and truth claims that are thrown at us. A Christian in a college setting may be fearful of ridicule or embarrassment and choose not to engage in critically evaluating the professor's claims. Professors often respond very aggressively to the first student to challenge their truth claims by seeking clarification or demanding supporting evidence. This is done purposely as a warning to anyone else who may be considering doing the same. Students are seldom willing to express their disagreements with the professor's position verbally or in writing because they fear its effect on their grades. Other emotions or "passions" have similar effects on our ability to think critically and engage the truth claims that cross our paths.

CONFORMITY: JUST "GOING WITH THE FLOW" TO DO THE POPULARLY DONE THING RATHER THAN THINKING THINGS THROUGH.

Conformity is directly related to peer pressure. Everyone longs to be liked and accepted by their peers. This often translates into an unwillingness to think clearly about the consequences of engaging in behaviors or agreeing to ideas that we would never even consider—were we thinking critically. This obstacle affects our ability to evaluate critically both the things we do and the ideas we embrace.

Have you ever consented and done something just to "go with the flow" that you later regretted? Too often we hear stories of kids getting in the car with a drunken teen behind the wheel because they were part of a group and did not want to be the oddball. The thought goes something like this: "if the rest of my friends were doing it, how could I say no?" In that decision point in the young person's life, instead of thinking critically about the potential for an accident or worse, the desire for acceptance and the pressure to conform override common sense. Sadly, we hear these stories when we wake up in the morning and the news headlines tell a shocking story of an accident with fatalities. Conformity also shows up in our commitment to ideas that are popularly accepted by our peers. Rather than take a position on an issue based on careful consideration of all the relevant information, people often adopt the position of their peers. Usually this results from a desire to fit in and/ or not stand out.

> **RATHER THAN TAKE A POSITION ON AN ISSUE BASED ON CAREFUL CONSIDERATION OF ALL THE RELEVANT INFORMATION, PEOPLE OFTEN ADOPT THE POSITION OF THEIR PEERS.**

PERSONAL COMMITMENT: AFFINITY, LOYALTY AND AFFECTIVE INVOLVEMENT WITH PARTICULAR INDIVIDUALS AND CLIQUES

Personal relationships are another common obstacle to critical thinking. Many people are unwilling to critically evaluate an idea or truth claim if it is presented by a close friend, a parent, or someone with whom we are emotionally bonded. Behind this obstacle lies the desire to be loyal and/or supportive of those we are close to. Rejecting their ideas or truth claims feels like a betrayal of the relationship. Thus, it is easier to simply accept a claim without much consideration for the sake of the relationship.

IDEOLOGICAL OR POLITICAL ALLEGIANCES

Nowhere is critical thinking abandoned more often than in politics. Being a good _____ (Republican, Democrat, etc.) means sticking to the party lines. If the party affirms Truth Claim A, than I don't even need to evaluate it, I just affirm it as well. Questioning or engaging in any type of critical thinking is seen as a betrayal of the party. This type of mind clouding is also manifest in political discourse. People have a tendency to reject any critical evaluations of their favorite politicians. It's as if their favorite politician can do no wrong.

In many cultures, political or ideological allegiances are a family thing. As a son of Cuban immigrants, I grew up in a "republican" home where my older brothers and my mother would always be instructed by my dad as to who they should vote for. Interestingly, candidates were always chosen down strict party lines. While there is nothing wrong with getting advice from one's parents, it is important to carefully consider the issues and come to our own educated decisions.

PERSONAL BIAS: GIVING CREDIT OR DISCREDIT BY APPRECIATION OR "SYMBOLIC"CONNECTION RATHER THAN ON MERIT

Personal biases have a tendency to adversely affect objectivity. While it is important to understand that nobody can escape their own personal biases completely, being aware of them and their potential to override objectivity helps the critical thinker minimize their effect. It is a sign of maturity in thinking to be able to critically evaluate even those ideas we hold dear. Particularly as Christians, we should evaluate the doctrines and teachings that we are exposed to, even if these ideas come from other Christians. When we fail to do so we often find ourselves recycling ignorance. A critical thinker understands that people (including other Christians) aren't perfect. The best theologian, pastor, Sunday School teacher, or professor can make a mistake in his/her interpretation of the Bible. This can be caused, among other reasons, by carelessness in Bible study, faulty reasoning leading to the adoption of particular ideas, their own personal biases, or any of the reasons presented in this chapter. That is why it is imperative that we continuously engage in critical thinking

"WISHFUL THINKING": BEING GUIDED BY OUR OWN DESIRES AND CONVENIENCES RATHER THAN BY EVIDENCE AND ARGUMENT

Sometimes an idea or truth claim can be very desirable or beneficial to the person considering it. When this is the case, it is easy to overlook the weaknesses or problems with an idea. The tendency is to focus exclusively on the positive. This can be very dangerous because we can find ourselves taking a position or adopting an idea that is detrimental to us physically, emotionally, or spiritually. Numerous dangerous, false, and non-biblical ideas have gained much popularity lately, precisely because of this "wishful thinking" problem. One such idea is the doctrine that everyone ends up in heaven. This sounds like a great idea. After all, don't we all wish that everyone in our families and all of our friends would go to heaven? Besides, wouldn't that be the perfect solution to the problem of a loving God sending anyone to hell? However, no amount of wishful thinking, nor the attractiveness of the idea makes it true. The Bible is clear in its teachings that some will not make it into heaven. In addition, a critical analysis of the idea itself would render it untenable.

Just think about how that doctrine eliminates divine justice. Or consider the number of people who don't want to be in heaven. Although God desires that all be saved (1 Timothy 2:4 & 2 Peter 3:9), He does not force anyone to accept the gifts of salvation and eternal life.

Even more popular today is the erroneous idea that all morality is relative to the individual; that everyone decides for himself what is right and what is wrong. This too sounds like a great idea. After all wouldn't we love to be able to do whatever we want and have it be good and acceptable before God? Yet, upon closer examination, this idea also proves to be untenable. Consider that if everyone decides for themselves what is right and wrong, then Adam and Eve did nothing wrong when they partook of the forbidden fruit. Thus, there never really was a sin problem, and Christ did not have to come and die on a cross. Furthermore, consider the internal contradictions and inconsistencies of this idea. On the one hand the proponent of such a truth claim celebrates everyone's right to do whatever they consider right while complaining that it is wrong for people to cut down trees, steal identities, or traffic children. They do this without having any rationally consistent grounds upon which to condemn such acts. A critical thinker will realize that the idea fails careful consideration, for God has established an objective moral standard of what is right and what is wrong and gives us the basis upon which we can condemn some behaviors and celebrate others.

While this list is not exhaustive, it gives the critical thinker much to think about. We must constantly strive to overcome these obstacles in the pursuit of truth. Furthermore, as Christians, we have nothing to fear when engaging in critical thinking. The truth always has a way of surfacing and winning the day.

CHAPTER 4

CRITICAL THINKING AND PHILOSOPHY

4

Critical thinking is a key component of the method of philosophy. When philosophers approach an open question, there are four steps that are typically taken in tackling the issue and pursuing a rational response. Each step is critical and is a pre-requisite to the next step. You cannot begin hypothesizing without first clarifying the concepts. You cannot test the possible hypothesis unless you have actually listed them.

1. *CLARIFYING CONCEPTS*
2. *HYPOTHESIZING*
3. *TESTING HYPOTHESIS*
4. *JUDGING POSSIBLE RESPONSES*

STEP 1: CLARIFYING CONCEPTS

You cannot engage a question that you don't understand. A critical thinker requires good definitions for the key concepts in an argument. However, when we engage in philosophy, there is more to clarification than defining concepts. In a philosophical approach to a proposition, we seek clarity in how the concepts are related one to the other. Specifically, we seek to find whether the concepts under consideration relate as Necessary Conditions or as Sufficient Conditions. Sometimes the concepts don't even relate. To the non-philosopher, these concepts are somewhat difficult to understand; but to the philosopher they are indispensable tools of the trade. Critical thinkers can also benefit tremendously from mastering these concepts.

> *A relationship under Necessary Conditions is defined as:*
>> *A condition q is necessary for p if it is impossible for something to be p without being q.*

> *A relationship under Sufficient Conditions is defined as:*
>> *A condition q is sufficient for p if it is impossible for something to be q and not p.*

To understand the difference between the two conditions, a diagram may help. Consider the following diagram and the explanation that follows:

ANIMALS	
COW	HORSE
DOG	FISH

What is the relationship between the concepts of fish and animals? If these two concepts are related, we can say that being an animal is a necessary condition for being a fish. That is, something has to be an animal if it is to be a fish. Conversely, we can also say that being a fish is a sufficient condition for being an animal. If you own a fish, you must also own an animal. In this example, animals is the broad category while fish is only one possible sub-set of that category.

Consider the following examples:
> To be a Junior in college is sufficient condition for being a college student since it is impossible that a Junior in college is not a college student.

On the other hand:
> Being a Junior in college is NOT a necessary condition for being a college student, since many college students are freshmen, sophomores or seniors.

Another way to explain necessary and sufficient conditions is to consider the if and only if perspective:

Q is necessary for P if and only if P can't occur without Q.

Whenever you have P, you have Q.

Anything P is Q.

$$P \longrightarrow Q$$
$$(P \text{ implies } Q)$$

Q is sufficient for P if and only if Q guarantees P.

Whenever you have Q, you have P.

Anything Q is P

$$Q \longrightarrow P$$
$$(Q \text{ implies } P)$$

Additional Example

By identifying the necessary and sufficient conditions we can better understand how concepts are related and more importantly how they are not. This will be very useful in identifying some of the fallacies that are common in argumentation.

Q	P	Condition
Being mortal	Being human	Q is necessary for P
Being female	Being pregnant	Q is necessary for P
Gas in car	Car runs	Q is necessary for P
Raining	Ground is wet	Q is sufficient for P
Getting an 80	Passing the class	Q is sufficient for P
Decapitation	Death	Q is sufficient for P

Table 1 Necessary vs Sufficient Cause

STEP 2: HYPOTHESIZING

Once all relevant terms or concepts have been clarified, we should have a clear understanding of the question being considered. The next step is to come up with a list of possible answers to the question. Each of these possible answers are called a hypothesis (a tentative explanation for a phenomenon, used as a basis for further investigation[2]). A key word for the philosopher at this stage is "possible." For the purpose of answering philosophical questions, we have to become familiar with two very different definitions of the word possible. Philosophers speak of things that are Causally Possible and things that are Logically Possible. By Causal Possibilities we mean that something is causally possible if it does not violate the laws of nature. It may be highly unlikely, but it must still be considered causally possible.

Consider the following examples:

> *It is causally possible for a blindfolded basketball player to hit 1,250 consecutive free throws.*

While this is highly unlikely, it does not violate any law of nature.

> *It is causally possible to see every red mustang convertible that drives through Manhattan in one afternoon.*

Again, this is highly unlikely, but it involves no violation of a natural law.

> *It is causally impossible for water to turn into gold.*

This claim is not causally possible because it violates the laws of chemistry.

> *It is causally impossible for the sun to rotate around the earth.*

This claim is not causally possible because it violates the laws of Astronomy and the laws of Physics.

Things that are causally possible must be considered as possible answers when evaluating alternatives. Claims that are causally impossible are usually excluded from the alternatives. However, if one is attempting to understand an event or claim where supernatural intervention has occurred, then causally impossible claims can be considered. If someone claims to have found a way to convert water into wine and wishes to sell the secret, a critical thinker would dismiss the claim due to the causal impossibility of the claim. However, when one posits a supernatural intervention, as in the miracle of Jesus converting water into wine, we are not describing an event governed by natural laws (that would be causally impossible), but rather an event that supersedes the laws of nature but falls well within the possibilities of an all-powerful God.

When considering Logical Possibilities we mean that something is logically possible when it does not entail a contradiction. Again, something may be highly unlikely, but we have to accept it as logically possible. It is also important to understand that something may violate a law of nature and still be logically possible, because it does not entail a contradiction.

Consider the following examples:

It is logically possible for the sun to rotate around the earth.

While that is not the way our solar system works, there is no contradiction in having a star like the sun orbiting around a planet like the earth. A good way to consider such scenarios is to ask ourselves if we can imagine a world in which it is the case. This is known as a thought experiment.

It is logically possible that all male faculty members at the University of Alabama are space aliens.

This scenario is logically possible because there is no inherent contradiction involved. Can you imagine a world in which this is true? If so, then it is logically possible.

> *It is logically impossible that a turtle is the creator of the universe.*

This claim is considered impossible because it involves an inherent contradiction. A turtle is part of the universe therefore it cannot be the creator of itself. By definition, anything that has a beginning must have been caused by something else.

> *It is logically impossible that everything came from nothing.*

Again this claim proves to be impossible because it involves an inherent contradiction. Nothing can bring forth nothing. From nothing one can expect nothing.

Logical possibilities are especially effective when evaluating claims of contradiction or impossibility. Sometimes people claim that something is impossible, when in fact it is logically possible because it involves no inherent contradiction. Skeptics often reject Jesus' deity because it would seem to be a contradiction—Jesus is either human or divine but cannot be both. In response, it is helpful to point out that there is no inherent contradiction in being human and being divine A dual nature may be unique and unprecedented but it is not contradictory. Others claim that God or his attributes are impossible and inherently contradictory.

It is not unusual for a skeptic to challenge a Christian with the following question as an attack on God's omnipotence, "Can God create a rock so heavy that he cannot lift it?" This is clearly a question of logical possibility vs. logical impossibility. In other words, if God can make a rock too heavy for him to lift, then he is not omnipotent. By the same token, if God can't make a rock too heavy for him to lift, then he is not omnipotent. Therefore, omnipotence is self-contradictory and God cannot be omnipotent. There are at least two problems with this claim.

First, by definition, something actually impossible cannot be done. In this case, God's omnipotence is irrelevant. Doing something that is actually impossible is not a matter of power. Making a square circle is not something that requires great power — it is something that cannot be done regardless of power. God can do whatever is possible and consistent with both His nature and the nature of the universe He created. After all, it was God himself who created this world in which certain things are impossible. The second problem pertains to the rock itself. In order for a rock to be "unliftable" by an infinitely powerful lifter, the rock would have to be infinitely heavy or infinitely large. But material objects, by definition, cannot be infinite; therefore, the infinite rock is self-contradictory.

The question is really asking if God can create a contradiction. The question is really asking if God can make a contradiction and the answer is NO. We could also add that God is not in the business of creating married bachelors or lifting himself by his bootstraps.

ONCE A CONTRADICTION IS FOUND IN A HYPOTHESIS, IT CAN BE DISCARDED.

When listing hypotheses, one need not include contradictions. Contradictions refer to statements or propositions that both affirm and deny that something is the case. Once a contradiction is found in a hypothesis, it can be discarded.

Consider the following contradictory statements:

- *He found a square circle.*
- *Carlos is a married bachelor.*
- *Jorge is taller than himself.*
- *He cannot turn both left and not left at the same intersection at the same time and in the same sense.*

All of these statements are clearly contradictory. By definition a square cannot be a circle. By definition a bachelor cannot be married. It is impossible to be taller than oneself. In addition, one cannot turn both left and not left at the same time and in the same sense. When these types of statements are found, they are a sure sign of error.

STEP 3: TESTING HYPOTHESES

Once a list of possible hypotheses has been identified the philosopher must engage in thought experiments. These are exercises in attempting to refute each hypothesis by finding logically possible scenarios that constitute counterexamples (a scenario that is incompatible with the truthfulness of the claim). Any claim or hypothesis that entails an internal contradiction or can be disproven by a counterexample is defective. It is a trait of good philosophy to find defective hypotheses and eliminate them. A thought experiment is when a philosopher imagines that the hypothesis is true and then tries to describe logically possible scenarios that are incompatible with the hypothesis being considered. **Think through the following claims:**

> *"If people lose their fear of hell, they will cease going to church."*

In order to disprove or reject this hypothesis one must be able to imagine a scenario that is logically possible and that counters the claim.

Can you imagine a person that goes to church and does not fear hell? I know many people who go to church because they love God and not because they fear hell. Each one of them is a counterexample that proves this statement is defective.

> *"It is impossible to survive the death of one's physical body."*

In order to disprove or reject this hypothesis one must be able to come up with a counterexample (someone who has survived the death of their physical body).

The Bible lists several people who were dead and then were miraculously resurrected including Lazarus and Jesus himself. These are counterexamples.

Furthermore, every day in hospitals people die and are brought back by medical procedures to revive them. These are also counterexamples that invalidate the claim.

> *"Consciousness is a basic requirement for being human."*

In order to disprove or reject this hypothesis one must be able to come up with a counterexample (someone who is not conscious and yet is still considered human).

There are many people who are in comas due to accidents or medical conditions and are thus completely unconscious. However, no one questions their humanity.

If a counterexample cannot be found and there appears to be no contradiction, the claim must be considered a possible response.

STEP 4: JUDGING POSSIBLE RESPONSES

Once the testing phase is complete, the philosopher is usually left with several competing and often contradictory hypotheses that can possibly provide the answer being sought. It is important to remember that they can all be wrong or one of them can be correct, but they cannot all be the right answer. The final step in philosophical method is to try to judge which possible hypothesis provides the most reasonable solution in light of all the available evidence. This is the most controversial step since it requires that we construct and evaluate a wide range of arguments in defense of, or in opposition to, various possible solutions. Furthermore, it is quite difficult (if not impossible) for the philosopher to be completely objective in his judgment. In order to make the best choice, the philosopher then proposes a logical argument in support of his decision.[3]

DEDUCTIVE ARGUMENTS: GENERAL

5

> *ALL PEOPLE MAKE MISTAKES AND I AM A PERSON.*

> *THAT MEANS YOU MAKE MISTAKES.*

Fred loves to argue! He argues with his wife, with his students, with his friends, with strangers, and with anyone who is willing to engage him. However, before we dismiss him as the type of person we never want around (i.e., always angry, obnoxious, irritating, close-minded) it would be helpful to clarify what an 'argument' is from Fred's perspective. An argument can be defined in terms of quarreling, fighting, yelling or bickering—the common meaning in everyday conversation. However, in a philosophical context, the word argument refers to *the logical discussion and/or evaluation of propositions and the evidence provided in their support.*

In this chapter we consider the word in light of the second definition—where a person or group engages in critical thinking regarding a proposition or claim. It is also important to note that there are 'rules of engagement' that help us in the process of evaluating propositions or claims. For this we turn to the field of logic.

LOGIC

Logic can be defined as the field of study that clarifies how we can distinguish good arguments from bad ones. Another excellent definition is provided by Norman Geisler & Ron Brooks: "Logic is a way to think so that we can come to correct conclusions by understanding implications and the mistakes people often make in thinking."[1] Thus, logic and critical thinking go hand in hand. Critical thinking and logic are used to evaluate truth claims, which usually appear as arguments. But, not all arguments are equally good. Many arguments that we find in everyday discourse are actually quite misleading, weak, or simply false.

A key to understanding and evaluating arguments is being able to identify the parts of an argument. Arguments have two basic components. The central component of an argument is the proposition or truth claim that is made. These propositions are statements that claim something is true or false and are commonly referred to as a conclusion. Simple arguments have one conclusion. Identifying the conclusion of an argument in everyday conversations requires some practice, but there are key words that point us in the right direction.

Conclusions often begin with one of the following indicators:

therefore	hence	consequently
thus	as a result	in conclusion
accordingly	so	it follows that
wherefore	for this reason	this implies that

The following examples illustrate how some of these indicators may appear in an argument:

> You want people to be kind to you, so be kind to them.
>
> People always lie to me; therefore people are not trustworthy.
>
> My car is always broken and very unreliable; consequently I have a bad car.
>
> Everyone is failing my chemistry class; this implies that the teacher is not very good.

These words indicate that what follows is to be considered a truth claim. The second component of the argument is the set of premises that support the conclusion. These are statements that are offered as proofs or evidence that the conclusion is true. Premises often have key words and phrases that make them easier to identify. Some of the most common are:

since	seeing that	inasmuch as
because for	considering that	
given that	judging from	as indicated by
as	on account of	

The following examples illustrate how some of these indicators may appear in an argument:

> *Seeing that students cheat on tests...*
>
> *Because forest fires are usually started by smokers...*
>
> *Considering that Rolex watches are very expensive...*

So how do the premises and conclusions come together? The following examples illustrate how premises and conclusions come together to form an argument:

EXAMPLE 1

Since [premise] cars are fast and

given that [premise] many people have accidents

it follows that [conclusion] cars are dangerous.

EXAMPLE 2

Considering that [premise] John is tall and [premise] John's father is tall, we may conclude [conclusion] that John's brother Peter will also be tall.

It is important to remember that premises don't always have indicator words. In those cases we can identify the premises because they are statements offered as evidence or reasons why we should accept another statement (the conclusion). In the same way, conclusions don't always have indicator words. In those cases we can identify the conclusion because it is the statement the premises attempt to prove or support.

Conclusions are a dime-a-dozen. Everyone has opinions of what is true and what is not. Everyone has beliefs that require evidence. However, the supporting premises that lead to those conclusions are a bit more difficult to find. Look at the following conclusion and see if you can come up with a set of premises that would support it:

"It is wrong to torture animals."

While most people would agree with this conclusion, coming up with two supporting premises can be challenging. One might argue that: Since it is cruel to torture animals and since cruelty is wrong, it follows that it is wrong to torture animals.

While this argument may sound good, it may or may not be a good argument. In the next section we will evaluate it further.

It is also important to understand the formal way of expressing arguments. A simple argument, often called a syllogism, consists of two premises and a conclusion as follows:

PREMISE 1

It is cruel to torture animals

PREMISE 2 That which is cruel is wrong

CONCLUSION:

Therefore, it is wrong to torture animals

Unfortunately for the critical thinker, people don't speak in syllogisms. Being able to identify the parts of an argument in everyday dialogue can be difficult. Consider, for example, the following argument and put it in standard form:

Only those beings are free who can act in unpredictable ways. It is thus obvious that robots can never be free, for robots are programmed to act in predictable ways.

If we ask ourselves what is being 'proven' we will find the conclusion: CONCLUSION: It is thus obvious that robots can never be free.

That leaves us with two statements that could be considered premises. The order of the premises is also important since we are "building" an argument for the conclusion. The premises would line-up as follows:

PREMISE 1

Only those beings are free who can act in unpredictable ways.

PREMISE 2

Robots are programmed to act in predictable ways.

CONCLUSION:

It is thus obvious that robots can never be free.

Furthermore, in everyday discourse we often find more information than is necessary for an argument. We find that some premises are implied, rather than stated. We also find that the arguments aren't always expressed in the proper order. Thus it becomes challenging to isolate and accurately determine what is being concluded and what is being argued in support of the conclusion. Take for example the following argument from an ordinary dialogue:

Our proposal was not accepted, since all proposals in the red folder were rejected.

What is the implied premise and what is the conclusion? In order to find it, it is helpful to put the argument in standard form first.

PREMISE 1   _____

PREMISE 2   All proposals in the red folder were rejected

CONCLUSION: therefore, our proposal was not accepted

What is the missing premise that is implied?

Our proposal was in the red folder.

With the basic components of argumentation out of the way, let us consider the two most common classifications of arguments. These are known as deductive and inductive arguments. In this chapter and the next we cover Deductive and Inductive Arguments and some of the variety within each type.

DEDUCTIVE ARGUMENTS

A deductive argument is one that if the premises are true, the conclusion must be true as well. Thus this type of argument attempts to prove—absolutely and undeniably, that the conclusion is true. An often cited example of a deductive argument is:

PREMISE 1   All humans are mortal.

PREMISE 2   Socrates is human.

CONCLUSION: Therefore, Socrates is mortal

Once the premises are established as true, the conclusion must follow. The key for the critical thinker is to be able to evaluate these arguments to determine if in fact they prove the conclusion absolutely and undeniably.

EVALUATING DEDUCTIVE ARGUMENTS

Evaluating deductive arguments requires that we consider both the structure of the argument and the truthfulness of the premises. When we consider the structure of the argument we can expect good deductive arguments to be valid. To say that an argument is valid means that if all the premises of the argument are true, then the conclusion must be true also. However, it is important to remember that validity has to do with the logical relationship between the premises and the conclusion—not with the veracity of the premises. An argument can be valid even if its premises are absolutely false. For example, consider the following valid deductive argument:

PREMISE 1   All circles are triangles.

PREMISE 2   All triangles are square.

CONCLUSION: Therefore, all circles are square.

AS IS TRUE OF ALL DEDUCTIVE ARGUMENTS, IF THE PREMISES ARE TRUE, THAN THE CONCLUSION MUST ALSO BE TRUE.

This argument is obviously false, but it is nonetheless valid. Why? Because if the premises were true, then the conclusion must be true—thus it is structurally valid. It may seem like an exercise in futility to determine if an argument is valid, since that doesn't guarantee that the premises are true. We are usually more concerned with the truthfulness than we are with the structure. However, if we can demonstrate that an argument is invalid then we can dismiss the argument without any further consideration.

So what about the truthfulness of the argument? If an argument is both valid and the premises are found to be true, then we consider it a sound argument. A sound argument is one where the premises are true and the structure is valid. To produce such arguments ought to be the goal of every person engaged in critical thinking and philosophy.

MAIN ARGUMENT TYPES

Deductive arguments come in various common forms or types. Let us consider some of the common types. Let us first consider the Modus Ponens argument.

Modus Ponens
(LATIN FOR "MODE THAT AFFIRMS")

PREMISE 1	If p then q
PREMISE 2	p
CONCLUSION:	q

This type of argument consists of one conditional premise, a second premise that affirms the antecedent (the if part) of the conditional premise, and a conclusion that asserts as true the consequent (the then part) of the conditional premise.

Consider the following example:

PREMISE 1	If Carlos drives while he is drunk [antecedent], he is an irresponsible person [consequent].
PREMISE 2	Carlos drives while he is drunk, [affirming the antecedent]
CONCLUSION:	Therefore: Carlos is an irresponsible person. [asserting the consequent]

Consider a BIBLICAL example of the Modus Ponens argument concerning the impact of the resurrection of Jesus based on 1 Corinthians 15.

PREMISE 1	If Jesus rose from the dead, then our faith is not futile.
PREMISE 2	Jesus rose from the dead
CONCLUSION:	Therefore, our faith is not futile.

As is true of all deductive arguments, if the premises are true, then the conclusion must also be true. When presenting this argument, the debate will center on the veracity of Premise 2. Proving it requires further arguments based on the evidence. One line of argument may look like this:

PREMISE 1	If Jesus physically appeared to many after his death, then he must have risen from the dead.
PREMISE 2	Jesus appeared to over 500 people after his death
CONCLUSION:	Therefore, Jesus must have risen from the dead

Being able to present the arguments in this format allows us to focus on the key arguments that support a conclusion. In addition, this type of straight forward argument has the power to be very persuasive to the rational seeker. Let us now consider the Modus Tollens argument.

Modus Tollens
(LATIN FOR "MODE THAT DENIES")

PREMISE 1	If p then q
PREMISE 2	Not- q
CONCLUSION:	Therefore: not p

This type of argument consists of one conditional premise, a second premise that denies (or affirms as false) the consequent of the conditional premise, and a conclusion that denies the antecedent of the conditional premise.

Consider the following example:

PREMISE 1	If I am to pass the class, then I have to score higher than 70% on the test.
PREMISE 2	I scored a 63% on the test. [or I did not score higher than 70%]
CONCLUSION:	Therefore, I did not pass the class.

Consider a BIBLICAL example concerning the Lordship of Jesus as explained in Luke 6:46.

PREMISE 1	If Jesus is your Lord, then you have to do what he says.
PREMISE 2	You do not do what he says
CONCLUSION:	Therefore, Jesus is not your Lord.

Once again, if the premises are true then the conclusion must follow.

Let us now consider the Disjunctive Syllogism argument.

Disjunctive Syllogism
(OR ARGUMENT BY ELIMINATION)

PREMISE 1	Either p or q
PREMISE 2	Not- q
CONCLUSION:	Therefore: p

This type of argument usually consists of a premise with two options, a second premise denying one of the options, and a conclusion asserting the remaining option. The idea is to eliminate all of the options until one is left as the only possible answer.

Consider the following example:

PREMISE 1   Either the meeting is on Sunday,

                          or it is on Monday.

PREMISE 2   The meeting is not on Monday.
                          [or "the meeting is not on Sunday"]

CONCLUSION: Therefore, the meeting is on Sunday.
                          [Therefore, "the meeting is on Monday"]

Consider a BIBLICAL example of the Disjunctive Syllogism concerning allegiance to Jesus as found in Luke 11:23

PREMISE 1   Either Carlos is with Jesus or

                          he is against him.

PREMISE 2   Carlos is not with Jesus

CONCLUSION: Therefore, Carlos is against him.

Once again, if the premises are true than the conclusion must follow. Let us now consider the Hypothetical Syllogism argument.

Hypothetical Syllogism (OR CHAIN ARGUMENT)

PREMISE 1	If p then q
PREMISE 2	If q then r
CONCLUSION:	Therefore: If p then r

This type of argument consists of three conditional statements linked together as shown above.

Consider the following example:

PREMISE 1	If my book is missing, then I can't do my homework.
PREMISE 2	If I can't do my homework, then I will get a zero.
CONCLUSION:	Therefore, if my book is missing, then I will get a zero

Consider a BIBLICAL example of the Hypothetical Syllogism concerning salvation as found in Ephesians 2:8-9.

PREMISE 1	If you are saved by faith, then you are not saved by works
PREMISE 2	If you are not saved by works, then you cannot boast
CONCLUSION:	Therefore, if you are saved by faith, then you cannot boast

Once again, if the premises are true than the conclusion must follow.

The four deductive arguments covered in this chapter are very useful in presenting strong arguments that leave no room for reasonable dissent. The challenge for us is to find and develop these arguments from the Bible without altering the original intent of the passages utilized. When we engage in discussions of faith and the Bible with non-believers, it would benefit us greatly to have numerous deductive arguments at hand in order to persuade them. However, people often abandon reason when they are not willing to accept a proposed conclusion. It is not uncommon to find people in the biblical narrative rejecting the arguments of Christ and the apostles, regardless of their strength.

CHAPTER 6

DEDUCTIVE ARGUMENTS: CATEGORICAL SYLLOGISM

6

> CICI IS A DOG, AND ALL DOGS ARE ANIMALS.

> THEN CICI MUST BE AN ANIMAL!

In addition to the four deductive arguments covered in the previous chapter, there is another very common argument type called Categorical Syllogism.

CATEGORICAL SYLLOGISM

PREMISE 1   All S are P.

PREMISE 2   All P are Q.

CONCLUSION: So, all S are Q.

The Categorical Syllogism is a three-line argument in which each statement begins with the word all, some, or no.

PREMISE 1   All poodles are dogs.

PREMISE 2   All dogs are animals

CONCLUSION: So, all poodles are animals

In order to understand, evaluate, and apply categorical syllogisms it is important that we consider the parts of a categorical statement or proposition as well as the classifications and implications of the categorical statement. As tedious as it may seem to some, the investment in learning this material will pay substantial dividends for the critical thinker.

A clear understanding of these parts is important to understand the proper structure of arguments. A categorical proposition is a "fact is fact" type of proposition, no "ifs", "ands", or "buts" about it. There are four parts to any categorical proposition:

1. The Subject term—the thing or thought about which the assertion is made.
Answers the question: What are we talking about?

2. The Predicate term—that which is asserted about the subject term.
Answers the question: What are we saying about it?

3. The copula—that which joins the subject and predicate terms.
An "is" or "is not" relational statement that connects the subject and predicate terms.

4. Quantifiers—the extent or number of the subject (all, some, none).

<u>Answers the question:</u> How much of it are we referring to?

When we put the four parts together, they look like this:

^{Quantifier} Subject ^{Copula} Predicate or

^{All} A ^{is} B

> *Examples:*
>
>> *"All dogs are animals"*
>>
>> *"Some students are intelligent"*
>>
>> *"No cars can fly"*

QUALITY AND QUANTITY

When the subject and predicate change, the content of a proposition also changes. However, the basic structure or pattern does not change. Nevertheless when the copula and quantifiers change, they can make a significant difference in the pattern of the propositions. Changing the "is" to "is not," or the "some" to "all," changes the type of proposition in a very significant way. When the copulas change, we call it differences in quality. When the quantifiers change, we call it differences in quantity.

The copula of any proposition can be either positive or negative. It either affirms or denies the relation between the subject and the predicate. It can say "is" or "is not," "was" or "was not," "will be," "will not be," "are," or "are not." We classify these <u>qualities</u> as affirmative or negative.

If the proposition says "All dogs are animals" it is affirmative.
If the proposition says "Man is not an animal" it is negative.

The quantifiers make a proposition either universal (all) or particular (some). The quantifier of the subject is what we must take note of; the predicates usually don't have one. If the proposition is referring to all things that can be included in the subject, it is called universal. It is common for universal propositions to have the word all or no at the beginning. If the proposition is only referring to part of the subject group, it is called particular. It is common for particular propositions to start with words like some and not all. Generally, if no quantifier is given, we assume that the proposition is universal.

Consider the following examples of the form and content of both Universal and Particular proposition.

Universal propositions: All S is P, or No S is P.
"All birds have feathers."
"No one is reliable."
"Dogs bark at strangers"

Particular propositions: Some S is P, or Some S is not P.

"Some stores are expensive."

"Some doctors are not cardiologists."

"Some cardiologists don't care about their patients."

QUALITY AND QUANTITY

These changes in quality and quantity can be classified into four types of propositions as follows:

Type A: Universal affirmative:	All S is P
Type E: Universal negative:	No S is P
Type I: Particular affirmative:	Some S is P
Type O: Particular negative:	Some S is not P

These four types exhaust all the possibilities.

DISTRIBUTION OF TERMS

Categorical syllogisms, as the name implies, are useful with placing things in the categories where they belong. It is vital to distinguish when we are referring to all of a category and when we are referring to only part of it. A term is distributed when it refers to all the members of its class. Distribution is usually identifiable by the use of the word "all" or the implication of it. Distribution applies to both the subject and the predicate. It is easy to memorize Distribution, because it is always the same for each of the four types of proposition.

Type A—All S $_{\text{DISTRIBUTED}}$ is P $_{\text{UNDISTRIBUTED}}$.

Let's use "cars" for the subject and "motor vehicles" for the predicate:

"All cars are motor vehicles."

The subject is distributed because all is stated. But is the predicate distributed? Is it referring to all motored vehicles? Of course not since motorcycles, mopeds, trains and airplanes are not included, it only covers the ones mentioned in the subject (cars). Thus it is undistributed. So the subject is always distributed and the predicate is always undistributed in Type A propositions.

Type E—No S $_{\text{DISTRIBUTED}}$ is P $_{\text{DISTRIBUTED}}$.

"No cars are two-wheeled vehicles."

Once again, the subject is distributed because it applies to all of its members—so this is a universal proposition. But what about the predicate? Does it refer to all or some two-wheeled vehicles? Here we are denying

IT IS VITAL TO DISTINGUISH WHEN WE ARE REFERRING TO ALL OF A CATEGORY AND WHEN WE ARE REFERRING TO ONLY PART OF IT.

that any of the subject is part of the predicate. In other words what the statement really says is, "None of all the cars in the world are included in all the two-wheeled vehicles in the world. Thus both subject and predicate are always distributed in Type E propositions.

Type I —Some S $_\text{UNDISTRIBUTED}$ is P $_\text{UNDISTRIBUTED.}$

"Some table tops are round."

The subject is always undistributed when we consider particular statements. But is the predicate distributed? Does it refer to all or some, to all round things or some round things? The predicate can only be undistributed. The most they can claim is that "Some table tops are some of the round things in the world." There are other round things, like cushions and quarters, and other table tops are not round. Thus Type I propositions always have undistributed subjects and undistributed predicates.

Type O—Some S $_\text{UNDISTRIBUTED}$ is not P $_\text{DISTRIBUTED.}$

"Some table tops are not round."

Again the subject is always undistributed when we consider particular statements. But is the predicate distributed? Does it refer to all or some, to all round things or some round things? This type of proposition is denying that some of the subjects are part of the predicate. By denying that something is inside a certain circle, you have to deny that it can be found anywhere in that circle. Thus Type 0 propositions always have undistributed subjects and distributed predicates.

PARTS OF A SYLLOGISM

The relationships between the statements are also very important. Premise 1 is known as the "major premise." Premise 2 is known as the "minor premise" and is the weaker of the two premises. Each of the premises and the conclusion has two slots for terms (subject and predicate). However, there can be no more than three unique terms to fill all six subject and predicate slots. There is the major term, the minor term and the middle term that serves as a bridge connecting the two premises.

Consider the following example:

PREMISE 1   Major premise
All the books in the Bible (middle term) are inspired by God (major term).

PREMISE 2   Minor premise
Jonah (minor term) is a book in the Bible (middle term).

CONCLUSION:
Jonah (minor term) is inspired by God (major term).

Notice the following:

There are only three unique terms in the six slots provided: all the books in the Bible, Inspired by God, and Jonah.

The major term must appear in the major premise and becomes the predicate of the conclusion.

The minor term must appear in the minor premise and becomes the subject in the conclusion.

The middle term appears in both major and minor premises—making the logical connection between the major and minor terms—but it does not appear in the conclusion.

Building on these observations we can establish six rules to assure us that the syllogism is valid (whether it is true or not). These rules are critical in putting together good arguments.

SIX RULES OF THE CATEGORICAL SYLLOGISM

1. There must be only three terms. When a syllogism contains four terms, it guarantees that there is NO connection between Premise 1 and Premise 2 and therefore, NOTHING can be concluded from the argument.

| Premise 1 | All S is P | | Premise 1 | All dogs are animals |
| Premise 2 | All M is R | | Premise 2 | All circles are round |

| *Therefore* | ?? | *Therefore* | ?? |

Because this is rather obvious, sometimes a fourth term sneaks into a syllogism by switching the meaning of terms between the first and second time it appears. This is called equivocation.

Consider the following example:

PREMISE 1	All algebra problems are hard.
PREMISE 2	All rocks are hard.
CONCLUSION:	Therefore, all rocks are algebra problems.

The problem with this syllogism is that "hard" in the first premise does not mean the same as "hard" in the second premise. In Premise 1, the term refers to something that is difficult. In Premise 2, it is referring to something that is rigid.

2. The middle term must be distributed at least once. The middle term is the bridge that connects both premises. This allows the conclusion to explain how the two premises are related to each other. If the middle term doesn't refer to its entire category at least once, there may not be any relation at all between the two premises.

Consider the following example:

PREMISE 1
All Men [Distributed] are of the talking kind [Undistributed.]

PREMISE 2
All Women [Distributed] are of the talking
kind [Undistributed.]

CONCLUSION:
Therefore, all Women [Distributed] are Men [Undistributed]

The "bridge" between the major and minor terms must be large enough (distributed—referring to all the members of a group) in order to connect the two terms. The middle term (in this case, the talking kind) needs to refer to the whole of some group before we can conclude that the sub-groups are included.

In order to understand this better, it is often helpful to consider a diagram.

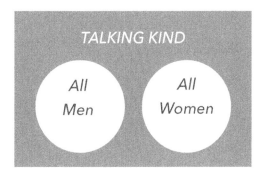

All men are part of Talking Kind

All women are part of Talking Kind

Conclusion: ???

The bridge "Talking Kind" is Undistributed in both Premise 1 & 2 therefore no conclusion is possible.

Consider an argument that is correctly distributed:

All men[dist] are mortal[undist]

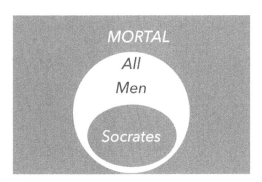

Socrates[dist] is a man[undist]

Socrates[dist] is mortal[undist]

The bridge "men" is Distributed in Premise 1 thus a conclusion is possible.

3. Terms distributed in the conclusion must be distributed in the premises. You can't get 10 lbs. of coffee from a 1 lb. bag.

Consider the following example:

PREMISE 1	All Christians are intelligent (a part of the intelligent group).
PREMISE 2	No Atheist is a Christian.
CONCLUSION:	Therefore, no Atheist is intelligent (the whole intelligent group).

You cannot go from a part of the intelligent group as your major term in premise 1 to all of the intelligent group in the conclusion. If we use an analogy of an eight drawer dresser, premise 1 tells us that all Christians are in drawer 3 of the intelligence dresser. Premise 2 tells us there are no atheists in drawer 3. However, the conclusion tells us there is no atheist in any of the 8 drawers. While that may be true or false, we cannot reach that conclusion from the relationship established in premises 1 and 2 because we are never told what is in the other drawers.

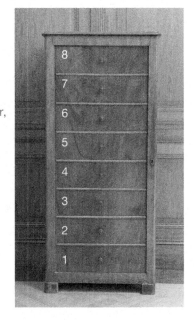

4. The conclusion always follows the weaker premise. If either premise 1 or premise 2 is particular (some), the conclusion must be particular. Likewise, if one of the premises is negative, the conclusion must be negative.

Consider the following example:

PREMISE 1 (Major)	No blind men are able to see. (universal/negative)
PREMISE 2 (Minor)	Some Hindus are blind men. (particular/affirmative)
CONCLUSION:	Therefore, some Hindus are not able to see. (particular/negative)

Since the major premise is negative, the conclusion must be negative as well. Since the minor premise is particular, the conclusion must be particular as well. Thus, the conclusion must be a particular negative statement (Type O).

5. No conclusion follows from two negative premises. In order for one group to have anything in common with another group, at least one of the premises has to be affirmative. Otherwise, there is nothing you can say about the two groups in common.

Consider the following example:

PREMISE 1   No dogs are baseball players.

PREMISE 2   No baseball players are short.

CONCLUSION: Therefore, ?

6. No negative conclusion follows from two affirmative premises. If both premises are affirmative, then the weakest possible conclusion is still affirmative. There is no way to sneak a negative into the conclusion if it wasn't there in the premises.

Consider the following example:

PREMISE 1   All squares are four-sided

PREMISE 2   Windows are square

CONCLUSION: Therefore, not all windows are four-sided

No negative conclusion can come from affirmative premises. Both premises 1 and 2 are affirmative, thus the negative conclusion does not follow. The conclusion ought to be "Windows are four-sided."

POSSIBLE COMBINATION OF TERMS EXAMPLES

Because of the wide variety of ways this type of argument can be expressed, it is critical to understand each component and how it affects the significance of what is being argued.

Premise 1 (Major Premise)	Middle/**MAJOR**
Premise 2 (Minor Premise)	**MINOR**/Middle
Conclusion	MINOR/MAJOR

P1 All men are **MORTAL**
P2 **SOCRATES** is man
Conc. SOCRATES is MORTAL

Premise 1 (Major Premise)	**MAJOR**/Middle
Premise 2 (Minor Premise)	Middle/**MINOR**
Conclusion	MINOR/MAJOR

P1 **MORTAL** are all men
P2 One man is **SOCRATES**
Conc. SOCRATES is MORTAL

Premise 1 (Major Premise)	Middle/**MAJOR**
Premise 2 (Minor Premise)	Middle/**MINOR**
Conclusion	MINOR/MAJOR

P1 All men are **MORTAL**
P2 One man is **SOCRATES**
Conc. SOCRATES is MORTAL

Premise 1 (Major Premise)	**MAJOR**/Middle
Premise 2 (Minor Premise)	**MINOR**/Middle
Conclusion	MINOR/MAJOR

P1 **MORTAL** are all men
P2 **SOCRATES** is a man
Conc. SOCRATES is MORTAL

A good critical thinker is able to put an argument in standard form and then evaluate it based on content and structure. Becoming familiar with the six rules is also extremely helpful.

CHAPTER 7

INDUCTIVE ARGUMENTS

7

EVERY TIME I HAVE COFFEE LATE AT NIGHT, I'VE HAD A HARD TIME SLEEPING.

IS HAVING COFFEE LATE AT NIGHT BAD FOR SLEEP?

POSSIBLY.

The Inductive Argument is such that even if the premises are true, the conclusion is true only to a certain level of probability. Thus, this type of argument attempts to show that the conclusion is likely, plausible, or highly probable.

EVALUATING INDUCTIVE ARGUMENTS

The key to evaluating whether an inductive argument is good or not is to determine if the conclusion is established to a high or low degree of probability. We need not concern ourselves with the argument being valid. **Consider the following example:**

PREMISE 1   All the cars I have ever seen have four tires

CONCLUSION: Therefore, all cars have four tires.

Notice that even if premise 1 is true, the conclusion can be false; there may be cars with more than four tires or less than four tires the person has never seen. Also, notice that inductive arguments don't have to have the three-line format.

When evaluating inductive arguments the strength or weakness of the argument becomes the focus. Strong inductive arguments are those that establish their conclusion to a high degree of probability. Their conclusion is highly likely. On the other hand, weak inductive arguments are those that establish their conclusion only to a low degree of probability. Their conclusion is highly unlikely.

WHEN EVALUATING INDUCTIVE ARGUMENTS, THE STRENGTH OR WEAKNESS OF THE ARGUMENT BECOMES THE FOCUS.

MAIN TYPES OF INDUCTIVE ARGUMENTS

Inductive arguments come in many forms. The three most common are:

1. Enumerative Inductive Argument

2. Analogical Argument

3. Abductive Argument

Let us consider each type individually and look at examples of what both weak and strong arguments look like.

ENUMERATIVE INDUCTIVE ARGUMENT

Enumerative inductive arguments are based on generalizations derived from a sample population. From the sample population, a claim is made about the population as a whole. The format is as follows:

PREMISE 1   All observed "P"s have been "R"s..

CONCLUSION: Therefore: Probably all "P"s

                      everywhere are "R"s

The strength or weakness of the argument depends on the likelihood that the sample group represents the whole.

Consider the following examples:

WEAK EXAMPLE:

PREMISE 1   All cell phones I have ever had

                      lose reception easily.

CONCLUSION: Therefore: Probably all cell phones

                      everywhere lose reception easily.

Notice that this argument is weak because it is based on an accidental relationship. It just so happens that I have not had good luck with cell phones. Furthermore, five or six cell phones are not sufficient to be representative of all cell phones everywhere. Also, there may be other factors involved, such as interference or bad locations for reception.

STRONG EXAMPLE:

PREMISE 1   Everything I throw up in the air comes back down.

CONCLUSION: Therefore: everything everybody throws up in the air will come back down.

Notice that this argument is strong because it is based on "law-like" relationship. The conclusion is highly probable because it is based on the law of gravity.

PROBLEMS WITH ENUMERATIVE INDUCTIVE ARGUMENTS

There are two major problems to be considered when evaluating an Enumerative Inductive Argument. First, if the sampling is too small, the conclusion may well be a hasty generalization. Second, if the sampling is not truly representative of the whole, then the conclusion may be biased. Thus the effectiveness of the argument depends on a large enough and representative sampling.

ANALOGICAL ARGUMENT

Another popular type of inductive argument is based on the use of analogies. An Analogical Argument is one where two or more things are found to be similar in several respects leading to the conclusion that they must be similar in some further respect. Analogies are found in several formats.

FORMAT 1

PREMISE 1   Object A and object B are similar

PREMISE 2   Object A has characteristic P

CONCLUSION: Therefore, Object B probably has
                        characteristic P.

Consider the following example:

PREMISE 1   The human brain is like a computer.

PREMISE 2   Every computer can be repaired
                        when it fails.

CONCLUSION: Therefore: The human brain can
                        be repaired when it fails.

FORMAT 2

PREMISE 1   Object A has properties P1, P2, P3 and P4

PREMISE 2   Object B has properties P1, P2 and P3

CONCLUSION: Therefore, Object B probably has
                         property P4

Consider the following example:

PREMISE 1	Cars need fuel, need maintenance, are unique, and can be sold on ebay.
PREMISE 2	Humans need fuel, need maintenance and are unique.
CONCLUSION:	Therefore: humans can probably be sold on ebay

FORMAT 3

PREMISE 1	Object A has characteristic P
PREMISE 2	Object B has characteristic P
PREMISE 3	Object A has characteristic M
CONCLUSION:	Therefore, Object B probably has characteristic M.

Consider the following example:

PREMISE 1	Public schools are closed on Veteran's Day.
PREMISE 2	Private schools are closed on Veteran's Day.
PREMISE 3	Public schools are closed on Labor Day.
CONCLUSION:	Therefore: Private schools are probably closed on Labor Day.

This type of argument can be very powerful in philosophy. The strength of the argument is going to depend on the degree to which the compared items are really similar or not.

Consider the following examples:

WEAK EXAMPLE (FORMAT 2):

PREMISE 1   Humans can walk, run, eat, sleep, and write poetry.

PREMISE 2   Cats can walk, run, eat and sleep.

CONCLUSION: Therefore, Cats can probably write poetry.

Notice that the analogy fails because humans and cats are not very similar. Walking, running, eating and sleeping are similarities that many animals and humans share. However, the differences are far more significant. Furthermore, writing poetry is a unique ability of the human mind that sets it apart from other living beings.

STRONG EXAMPLE (FORMAT 1):

PREMISE 1   People are like puppies.

PREMISE 2   If you give puppies love and
              attention, they will be your friend
              for life.

CONCLUSION: Thus, if you give people love
              and attention, they will probably
              be your friend for life.

Notice that all analogies eventually fail. Otherwise, they would not be analogies, since an analogy is a comparison between objects that are ONLY SIMILAR, BUT NOT THE SAME. Thus, the effectiveness or strength of an analogy is dependent on the degree of similarity or difference in the specific area of comparison.

NOTICE THAT ALL ANALOGIES EVENTUALLY FAIL.

SEVEN STEPS IN EVALUATING ANALOGIES[1]

The following steps are very helpful in evaluating the strength of analogical arguments. **Consider the following argument:**

PREMISE 1   Tiffany and Heather are both tall
              and play basketball

PREMISE 2   Tiffany also plays volleyball.

CONCLUSION: So, Heather must also play volleyball.

This argument is clearly an example of the fallacy of weak analogy, but where does the reasoning fail? In order to evaluate the analogy there are certain steps we need to take.

STEP 1 Evaluate the Truth of the premises. If we find that either Tiffany or Heather doesn't play basketball or is not tall, then the argument falls apart.

STEP 2 Consider the relevance of the similarities. In the case of Tiffany and Heather the similarities are relevant because they make a difference as to whether the conclusion is likely to be true. The fact that they are both tall and athletes would seem advantageous to play volleyball. Sometimes similarities are irrelevant to the conclusion. If we were told that they are both women, both blond, and both had six letters in their name, the argument would be no stronger since these similarities are irrelevant to playing volleyball.

STEP 3 Consider the number of relevant similarities. This example only has two relevant similarities: they are tall and play basketball. If additional relevant similarities could be added, the argument would strengthen. If we knew that they were twin sisters who did everything together, the argument would be much stronger. If we knew that the basketball coach was also the volleyball coach and he demanded his athletes play on both of his teams, it would also strengthen the argument.

STEP 4 Consider the relevance of dissimilarities. Not all dissimilarities are relevant. Tiffany may be blond while Heather is a brunette. Tiffany may be left-handed while Heather is right-handed. None of these has any bearing on the strength or weakness of the argument. However, if Heather has to work a part-time job and Tiffany doesn't, that would weaken the argument significantly. Or if Heather does not like volleyball whereas Tiffany does, that would be devastating to the argument.

STEP 5   Consider the number of relevant dissimilarities. Obviously, the greater the number of relevant dissimilarities we find in an argument, the weaker it becomes. If it were true that Heather has to work a part-time job, hates volleyball, hates the volleyball coach, and has been forbidden to play volleyball by her parents, then the argument would become significantly weaker.

STEP 6   Consider the size of the sample group. In this argument we have a sample of only two (Tiffany and Heather). However, if we had a larger sample, it would increase the strength of the argument as well. If we argued,

PREMISE 1	Tiffany, Heather, Amber, and Krissy are tall and play basketball.
PREMISE 2	Tiffany, Amber, and Krissy also play volleyball.
CONCLUSION:	So, Heather must also play volleyball.

The argument would be stronger than the former because we have increased the sample size.

STEP 7   Consider the specificity of the conclusion relative to the premises. The broader and less specific the conclusion is, the stronger the argument is. In the volleyball argument, the conclusion is very narrow and specific, particularly considering the evidence offered by the premises. The strength of the argument would increase if the conclusion was "Heather must have played a game of volleyball at some time," or "Heather may also play volleyball."

ABDUCTIVE ARGUMENT

(Inference to the Best Explanation / Causal Argument)

Another popular form of inductive argument, often used by scientists, is based on observations and the search for cause and effect relationships. This argument requires the type of reasoning used by detectives. All of the relevant evidence and clues that surround an effect are considered in search for the cause of said effect. The question is what caused those clues to come into existence? Abduction can be defined as reasoning from effects back to causes. However, there are some limitations to Abductive arguments.

Consider the following example:

PREMISE 1	The street in front of my house was wet this morning.
PREMISE 2	When it rains, the streets get wet.
CONCLUSION:	Therefore, it rained on my street.

Can we infer that it rained? No. Why not? When we reason back to the cause from the effect we have to be careful because there may be more than one cause for that effect. Instead of rain, a fire hydrant may have broken, or a water main may have been damaged by a construction crew, or a helicopter carrying water to a nearby forest fire may have accidentally spilled its load on my street. In order to deal with that we must consider the multiple competing explanations in search for the BEST explanation.

So what makes an explanation the best one? The BEST explanation is the one that provides the most adequate CAUSAL explanation. Consider the wet street argument. A simple evaluation of the competing hypotheses clearly points to one explanation being the most probable.

EXPLANATION 1—A fire hydrant broke and flooded my street.

PROBLEM— I looked down the street and noticed that all of the fire hydrants seem in good condition and had no signs of leaking water.

EXPLANATION 2—A construction crew damaged a water main on my street causing it to flood.

PROBLEM—There is no construction happening on my street and there are no signs of any excavation anywhere on my street.

EXPLANATION 3—A helicopter accidentally spilled the water it was carrying to a forest fire.

PROBLEM—I don't live anywhere near a forest. Furthermore, to the best of my knowledge, there are no fires anywhere near my street.

While it is true that none of these problems are insurmountable, they render the explanation as highly unlikely. This leaves only one explanation that seems to fit all that I know and can observe: my street is wet because it rained.

BEST EXPLANATION: It rained on my street.

Consider another example of an Abductive argument:

PREMISE 1	I saw strange lights in the sky late last night.
PREMISE 2	The best explanation for these strange lights is that they are caused by alien spaceships.
CONCLUSION:	Therefore, aliens probably exist.

The strength of the arguments depends on the truthfulness of premise 2. A list of additional possible explanations might include shooting stars, asteroids, Air Force training exercises, hallucinogenic drugs, etc. But how can we determine whether a given explanation of an event is better than all other explanations? Two principles frequently play a prominent role:

Ockham's Razor:

An explanation A is better than explanation B if (all other things being equal) explanation A is simpler than explanation B.

EXAMPLE: If someone is looking for me at church and sees my car in the parking lot, the lights on in my office, and hears my voice through the closed door, the best explanation is that I'm in my office at church. However, that is not the only possible explanation. My car could be a holographic projection from an alien spacecraft hovering over the church. I may have forgotten to turn off the lights and the voice you hear is a digital recording. The alternative explanation is, however, far less likely and more complicated. Ockham's razor suggests that my being in my office is a simpler and thus better explanation.

WEAKNESS: The primary weakness of Ockham's Razor is that the true cause of a given effect can be far more complicated (less simple) than the alternative answers. This is often the case when considering scientific explanations.

The Principle of Conservatism:

An explanation A is better than explanation B if (all other things being equal) explanation A fits together better with the rest of my other beliefs about the world.

EXAMPLE: When considering the cause of the lights in the sky late at night, one's beliefs about the existence of aliens plays a primary role. If one believes that aliens don't exist, then the Principle of Conservatism would reject the explanation of alien spaceships causing the lights, since it would not fit well with one's beliefs.

WEAKNESS: The primary weakness of the Principle of Conservatism is that the evaluation of possible causes will always be limited by one's bias. What happens if one's beliefs about the world are wrong? What happens if the real cause falls outside of the parameters of what we believe possible? An excellent contemporary example of this is the strong commitment by some scientists today to the philosophy of Naturalism. This commitment excludes any non-natural explanation from the Scientific Method. Thus, when scientists are confronted with clear and obvious signs of intelligence in the design of life, they must posit a naturalistic explanation since their evaluation is biased in such a way as to exclude even the possibility of an intelligent cause behind creation. Thus, the strength of this principle is directly related to how well our beliefs correspond with reality.

While both principles are somewhat controversial, they can be helpful in eliminating possible causes and thus isolating probable causes. It is far easier to show that something couldn't be the cause than it is to prove what the cause of a given effect is.

In comparing deductive vs. inductive arguments, a critical thinker would always prefer a deductive argument because of its ability to "prove" the veracity of a statement. However, for many of the controversial topics that we face in everyday life, deductive arguments are not available. Otherwise, there would be no controversy and all of the issues would have been resolved. Thus, inductive arguments are far more common.

An important goal for a critical thinker is to be able to identify whether the argument being considered is deductive or inductive and then proceed to evaluate accordingly. When the critical thinker is the one presenting an argument, the goal must be to use deductive arguments (and use them properly) whenever possible and defer to inductive arguments only if necessary. Both the tasks of evaluating arguments and presenting arguments of our own require careful thought and consideration, but the results can be very rewarding.

The next three chapters deal with fallacies (errors in logic and argumentation) that often appear in arguments. Chapter 8 deals with fallacies of categorical syllogisms and is primarily focused on the "form" of the argument. Thus we call them Formal Fallacies. These fallacies can be a bit confusing at times and are often hard to understand. Chapters

9-10 deal with fallacies of content, setting, tone, etc, everything except form. Thus we call them Informal Fallacies. These fallacies are far easier to understand and to identify when they appear in an argument.

FORMAL LOGICAL FALLACIES

8

> I REALLY LOVE CHOCOLATE

> WHEN PEOPLE ARE IN LOVE THEY SHOULD GET MARRIED!

Logic and fallacies go hand in hand. Logic is a way of thinking that allows us to come to correct conclusions by understanding the mistakes people often make in thinking and arguing. Part of studying reasoning and logic is recognizing when P implies Q and when it doesn't. In order to accomplish this task there are clearly delineated rules that prescribe the correct form of arguments, as we observed in the previous chapters. There are also common ways in which people violate these rules of argumentation and logic. Mistakes in logic and argumentation are called fallacies.

Sometimes we are guilty of implying something that is not correct or structuring our arguments so that they are invalid. This category of mistakes has to do with the form of an argument and thus it is called Formal Fallacies. All other types of mistakes such as erroneous presuppositions, the use of irrelevant information, and the lack of clarity are grouped together loosely in what is often referred to as Informal Fallacies.

FORMAL FALLACIES

There are six major fallacies dealing with mistakes in the form of deductive arguments. These are divided in two groups. First there are four fallacies that are common to categorical syllogisms, and they include Illicit Major, Illicit Minor, Illicit Middle, and Four Term Fallacy. You will notice that these fallacies occur when one of the rules that appear at the end of Chapter 6 is violated. The second set consists of two fallacies common to hypothetical syllogisms, and they include Denying the Antecedent and Affirming the Consequent.

FALLACIES OF CATEGORICAL SYLLOGISM

ILLICIT MAJOR: This fallacy occurs when the major term is distributed in the conclusion but not in the premise. It involves an invalid use of the major term in the syllogism.

Consider the following example:

PREMISE 1	All [the girls in my first grade class]$^{Dist.}$ are [children]$^{Undist.}$
PREMISE 2	No [boys in my first grade class]$^{Dist.}$ are [girls in my first grade class]$^{Dist.}$
CONCLUSION:	No [boys in my first grade class]$^{Dist.}$ are [children]$^{Dist.}$

This argument is invalid because the major term, <u>children,</u> is undistributed in Premise 1 but distributed in the conclusion. In the first premise, "children" refers only to some members of the group of children (the girls in my first grade class). But when we arrive at the conclusion, "children" refers to the entire group of those who are children. You cannot logically conclude anything about a whole group of children from something you only know about part of the group. In this example it is obvious that the whole group of children consists of much more than girls in a given first grade class. Common sense tells us that boys in a first grade class are also children. However, we must be careful because sometimes the fallacy isn't that obvious.

ILLICIT MINOR:

This fallacy commits the same error as the previous one, but with the minor term instead of the major term. This fallacy occurs when the minor term is distributed in the conclusion but not in the premises. It involves an invalid use of the minor term in the syllogism.

Consider the following example:

PREMISE 1	All [the men in my family]$^{Dist.}$ are [Republican]$^{Undist.}$
PREMISE 2	All [the men in my family]$^{Dist.}$ are [Cubans]$^{Undist.}$
CONCLUSION:	All [Cubans]$^{Dist.}$ are [Republican]$^{Undist.}$

This argument is invalid because the minor term, <u>Cubans,</u> is undistributed in Premise 2 but distributed in the conclusion. In the second premise, "Cubans" refers only to some members of the group of Cubans (the men in my family). But when we arrive at the conclusion, "Cubans" refers to the entire group of those who are Cubans. You cannot logically assume that what is true about some members of the group Cubans is true of all the members of the group. Common sense tells us that not all Cubans are Republican simply because the men in my family are. As is the case with Illicit Major, we must be careful because sometimes the fallacy isn't that obvious.

ILLICIT MIDDLE:

This fallacy, also called Undistributed Middle, occurs when the middle term is not distributed at least once. It involves an invalid use of the middle term.

Consider the following example:

PREMISE 1   All [athletes][Dist.] are
              [health conscious] [Undist].
PREMISE 2   Peter [Dist.] is [health conscious] [Undist.]
CONCLUSION: Peter [Dist.] is an [athlete] [Undist.]

This argument is invalid because the middle term, "health conscious," is undistributed in both premises. In other words athletes are part of the group of the "health conscious," and Peter is also part of the group, but nothing in the argument suggests that Peter and Athletes are in the same part of the group.

In order for the argument to be valid, the middle term has to include both the major and the minor terms in a whole group (it must be distributed in at least one of the premises). Otherwise, there is no necessary connection between the major and minor terms. Peter may be an invalid octogenarian, who happens to be health conscious, but he is not, nor has he ever, been an athlete.

FOUR-TERM FALLACY:

This fallacy occurs when there are more than three terms in an argument. As was discussed previously—a typical three line syllogism can only have three unique terms.

Consider the following example:

PREMISE 1   All synthetic sugars are bad.

PREMISE 2   My girlfriend is bad.

CONCLUSION: My girlfriend is synthetic sugar.

It is invalid because the middle terms are different. Synthetic sugars are "bad" as in being unhealthy to consume, while My girlfriend is "bad" as in morally reprehensible or evil. Thus the very term that is supposed to connect the major and minor terms ends up separating them. There is no point of comparison between Premise 1 and Premise 2 from which we may draw any logical conclusion.

FALLACIES OF HYPOTHETICAL SYLLOGISMS
"DENYING THE ANTECEDENT"

This fallacy occurs when the causal relationship implied in Premise 1 is overly emphasized. In a typical hypothetical syllogism the antecedent (the if part) cannot be denied without invalidating the entire argument.

Consider the following example:

PREMISE 1   If Peter studies, then he will pass the test.
PREMISE 2   Peter didn't study
CONCLUSION: Peter will not pass the test.

While this argument may sound rational and valid—closer examination highlights the error in logic. Just because Peter studies (the antecedent) implies he will pass the test (the consequent) does not mean that passing the test cannot happen without studying. Something else may also cause the passing of the test. Peter may pass the test by making educated guesses. He may pass the test by cheating, or he may know the material and does not need to study. Furthermore, if the argument is attempting to demonstrate a cause/effect relationship between the antecedent and the consequent, denying the antecedent dismisses the whole proposition. You cannot draw conclusions or evaluate the relationship of a consequence to an event if it never happened. We will never know if studying caused him to pass the test since he didn't study.

Correction:

As we saw in Chapter 5, the Modus Ponens argument affirms the antecedent and thus leads to a logical conclusion. Consider what this looks like using the same example but affirming the antecedent.

> PREMISE 1   If Peter studies, then he will pass the test.
>
> PREMISE 2   Peter studied [affirming the antecedent]
>
> CONCLUSION: Peter will pass the test.

Affirming the Consequent:

As is the case with the previous fallacy, this fallacy occurs when the causal relationship implied in Premise 1 is overly emphasized. In a typical hypothetical syllogism affirming the consequent (the then part) does not necessarily affirm the antecedent.

Consider the following example:

> PREMISE 1   If the Apostle Paul was killed in a drive by shooting, then the Apostle Paul is dead.
>
> PREMISE 2   The Apostle Paul is dead.
>
> CONCLUSION: Therefore, the Apostle Paul was killed in a drive-by shooting.

Once again, this argument may sound rational and valid. However, upon closer examination, the error in logic becomes quite evident. Just because the Apostle Paul is dead (the consequent), it does not mean that his passing was the result of a drive-by shooting (the antecedent). Something else may have caused the death of the Apostle Paul. History both negates the given conclusion (guns and cars did not exist back then) and provides an alternative explanation for the death of the Apostle Paul—martyrdom.

Correction:

As we saw in Chapter 5, the Modus Ponens argument affirms the antecedent and thus leads to a logical conclusion. Consider what this looks like using the same example but affirming the antecedent.

PREMISE 1	If the Apostle Paul was killed in a drive by shooting, then the Apostle Paul is dead.
PREMISE 2	The Apostle Paul is not dead. [denying the consequent]
CONCLUSION:	Therefore, the Apostle Paul was not killed in a drive-by shooting.

While the formal logical fallacies considered in this chapter may be difficult to grasp at first, they are vitally important if we are to avoid error. Once these fallacies are mastered, evaluating formal arguments will be much easier and so will developing strong formal arguments.

INFORMAL LOGICAL FALLACIES PART 1

9

> *DON'T LISTEN TO HIS REASONING. HE IS A MEAN PERSON.*

> *YOU SHOULD LISTEN TO ME BECAUSE IF NOT, I'LL HURT YOU.*

It seems that humans can come up with an almost infinite number of ways to be mistaken. Aristotle listed thirteen informal fallacies, but some modern philosophers have listed and defined in excess of one hundred different ones. Furthermore, classifying or sub-dividing these fallacies can be a difficult task. There are almost as many different forms of subdividing the informal fallacies as there are fallacies. For our purposes we will divide informal fallacies into three major subdivisions: Fallacies of Relevance, Fallacies of Presumption, and Fallacies of Clarity.

FALLACIES OF RELEVANCE

This category includes a number of fallacies that in one way or another introduce irrelevant points and issues into the arguments. These are arguments where the premises have no bearing on the truth of the conclusions. The varieties of ways in which we can deviate from the relevant issues are almost endless, but let us consider the most commonly used of these fallacies. While most of these fallacies can be found easily in written form, some of them can also be found in verbal arguments (i.e., debates).

A subcategory of irrelevant arguments is known as Ad Hominem Attacks. These are attacks on a person, group, or circumstance. What makes these a fallacy is the fact that the attacks are irrelevant to the conclusion.

1.1 AD HOMINEM ABUSIVE:

This fallacy occurs when one party attacks the other with strong and abusive language in an attempt to avoid the main issue. It can also be found in syllogisms when one or both premises are attacks on the opponent but without any relevance to the conclusion.

Consider the following example:

EXAMPLE : "I don't think Peter is right about babies being defined as persons from the moment of conception, because he is an ignorant red neck. What does he know?"

ANALYSIS : This person's response to Peter's argument about person-hood beginning at conception fails to address the issue or present a relevant counterargument. They simply resort attacking Peter instead of the issue. It amounts to simple name calling.

1.2 AD HOMINEM CIRCUMSTANTIAL:

This fallacy occurs when certain circumstances are attacked in an attempt to invalidate the argument. It is a fallacy of relevance because the circumstances are irrelevant to the validity of the premises and the conclusion. The most common version of this fallacy attempts to invalidate an argument because the person presenting it stands to gain or benefit from the conclusion being true.

EXAMPLE : "I disagree with Julie's arguments for the reliability of the Bible because Julie is a fundamentalist Christian. Of course she is going to think the Bible is reliable."

ANALYSIS : This person's response to Julie's argument about the reliability of the Bible fails to address the issue or present a relevant counter-argument. They simply dismiss the argument because of Julie's commitment to the Christian faith. By calling her a "fundamentalist Christian" they avoid having to deal with the argument itself.

1.3 TU QUOQUE:

This fallacy occurs when the proponent of an argument is accused of not representing the conclusion of the argument. In other words, it's a "look who's talking" claim. The proponent of the fallacy argues that his rival's recommendations should not be accepted because he fails to follow it himself. Sometimes this fallacy is committed when someone attempts to justify or defend themselves of an accusation by claiming that their opponent has made the same error.

EXAMPLE : "Hey! How can you say that my running a red light is wrong when you do it all the time?"

ANALYSIS : How often one person runs or does not run red lights is irrelevant to the fact that it is wrong to run a red light. The "wrongness" can be based on the illegality of the act or on the possible tragic consequences of having an accident. In either case, the habits of the person pointing out the "wrongness" are irrelevant.

1.4 APPEAL TO FEAR:

This fallacy occurs when an argument attempts to persuade someone to accept a given position out of fear of the consequences of not doing so. While there may or may not be consequences, the consequences have no bearing on the truthfulness or validity of any given argument. Often, the consequences are exaggerated and not as severe as suggested.

EXAMPLE : "We must not allow God in the science classroom or it will be the end of modern science as we know it. Before long we will be in the dark ages again."

ANALYSIS : This is a common argument presented against the teaching of Creation Science or Intelligent Design in the science classroom. However, the decision to include or exclude such alternative views should be based on the truthfulness and validity of each, rather than on fear that it will have adverse consequences. Furthermore, this type of argument fails to establish a connection between teaching alternatives to Darwinian naturalism and the regress of science. Finally, the scenario presented is greatly exaggerated. Can anything we teach today make us as a society regress to the ignorance of the middle ages? It is highly doubtful.

1.5 APPEAL TO FORCE:

This fallacy occurs when someone attempts to persuade by force. It is reasoning through blackmail or by intimidation. This argument does not even try to address the topic from a rational or logical position. It is addressed instead from a position of strength.

EXAMPLE : "Mr. Blurgin, I should get an 'A' in your class because my dad, the Principal of the school, would be very upset if I don't, and by the way he is your boss. You may like to know that the last teacher who did not give me an 'A' is no longer teaching here."

ANALYSIS : This student's "reasoning" is fallacious because creating fear in people does not constitute evidence for a claim. There is no rational argument offered for the claim "I should get an

'A' in your class." Instead the student is blackmailing his teacher by threatening to get him fired if he does not agree with the claim, SINCE his dad is the Principal of the school.

1.6 MOB APPEAL / BANDWAGON ARGUMENT:

This fallacy occurs when an appeal is made to the emotions of the crowd or to that of the "common man." This fallacy is usually present where there is a lack of good arguments or sound reason. It's the now infamous "Joe the plumber" appeal. It is also used to convince the audience of the argument that everyone else believes something so they should join the bandwagon.

EXAMPLE : "Allison, you have to vote 'YES' on Amendment 7. Almost every student in our university is voting 'YES' on that amendment."

ANALYSIS : The problem with this argument is its failure to address any rational reason for voting in favor of a given issue. The number of students voting "YES" is irrelevant. History has shown us that the majority can be and often is wrong. The decision should be based on an evaluation of the relevant issues.

1.7 SNOB APPEAL:

This fallacy occurs when an attempt is made to persuade someone by appealing to a sense of elitism. It is an attempt to persuade someone not to be like everyone else, but rather to be a part of a select or "special" group.

EXAMPLE : "Intelligent people know that Neo-Darwinism is a fact. Only ignorant 'flat-earthers' question it. You, most definitely, don't want to be associated with those ignoramuses."

ANALYSIS : There are numerous problems with this common argument. First, it fails to address the rational reasons for accepting Neo-Darwinism or rejecting alternative views. Second, it fails to mention the growing number of Ph.D.s that are abandoning Neo-Darwinism as a model of origins. In addition, it implies erroneously that acceptance of Neo-Darwinism is a necessary condition of being intelligent. Furthermore, it also blatantly misrepresents opponents of Neo-Darwinism by suggesting they believe the earth is flat (more on this point in 1.9). Finally, the argument also commits the Ad Hominem fallacy by resorting to name calling instead of considering the arguments raised by the opponents.

1.8 APPEAL TO PITY / AD MISERICORDIUM:

This fallacy occurs when the proponent attempts to persuade others by making them feel sorry for themselves or someone else. A sense of pity or sympathy is supposed to override the validity of an argument.

EXAMPLE : "You cannot fire Bill. This job is the only thing he has left. He has lost his marriage, he is sick, and his dog died two days ago."

ANALYSIS : This argument fails because pity does not serve as evidence for a claim. The decision to fire or not fire Bill should be based on individual performance, company performance, budgetary issues, or other relevant factors.

1.9 STRAW MAN:

This fallacy occurs when someone draws a false picture of the opposing view in order to easily destroy the view. It keeps the proponent from having to deal with or even understand the real issues since he is responding to his own easy-to-refute version/ misrepresentation of the opposition's view.

EXAMPLE 1: Richard Dawkins, a modern atheist, refers to anyone who believes in creation as a "flatearther." Thus he can easily dismiss the view and not have to deal with the arguments.

ANALYSIS: He creates a misrepresentation of the creation view and then easily discredits it, since everyone knows the earth is not flat.

EXAMPLE 2: Atheists often paint a false picture of the Doctrine of the Trinity in order to dismiss God as a logical contradiction. They argue that Christians believe in a god that is defined as "3 Gods = 1 God." Everyone knows that 3 does not equal 1, thus such a god cannot exist; he would be the equivalent of a square circle.

ANALYSIS: In this argument the atheist misrepresents the biblical view of the Trinity in order to create a self-contradictory view that defeats itself. The Bible teaches that "3 Persons = 1 God" and there is no inherent contradiction there—mystery YES—contradiction NO.

EXAMPLE 3: Atheists often resort to a Straw Man Argument to dismiss the cosmolvogical argument for God's existence. They maintain that the argument fails because "if everything needs a cause, what caused God?"

ANALYSIS : The problem with this "straw man" is that the law of causality is misstated. The law of causality does not claim that everything needs a cause. Instead it says that every event or beginning needs a cause. God is obviously not an event. By definition God is; He doesn't happen.

1.10 RED HERRING:

This fallacy occurs when someone purposely diverts the attention from the topic at hand by using an irrelevant joke, anecdote, or by simply opening a discussion about a topic other than the one being argued. Instead of proving a point, he changes the subject and thus manages to evade the real issue being argued.

EXAMPLE : "Any measure that undermines the right to have an abortion must be rejected. There are too many hungry and abused children in this world already."

ANALYSIS : This argument fails to address the issues involved in the abortion debate (i.e., the definition of person-hood, when life begins, women's rights vs. the baby's rights, etc.) and focuses instead on an irrelevant issue. The number of hungry and abused children in the world is an entirely different point. Hunger and child abuse occurs in societies where abortion is legal and in societies where it is illegal. Furthermore, having the child or not having the child does not necessarily increase the problems of hunger or child abuse.

1.11 BEGGING THE QUESTION /CIRCULAR REASONING:

This fallacy occurs when the proponent introduces the claim that the conclusion is true in the premises of the argument. Whether it is expressed directly or indirectly, a claim that something is true cannot be considered evidence that it is true.

EXAMPLE :

Mary: *"I know God exists."*

Joe: *"How do you know?"*

Mary: *"The Bible says God exists."*

Joe: *"How do you know the Bible is telling you the truth?"*

Mary: *"Because it is God's word."*

ANALYSIS : While that claim that God exists is true, this argument presents no evidence in favor of the claim. An assumption cannot be used as reasonable evidence. One cannot assume that God exists and then use that assumption to prove it.

1.12 CHRONOLOGICAL SNOBBERY:

This fallacy occurs when a person appeals to the age of something in order to justify accepting it or rejecting it. There are two distinct approaches to chronological snobbery. When something "new" is painted in a positive light versus something "old" it is commonly known as Appeal to Novelty. This type of "reasoning" is very common for various reasons. First, our culture is heavily committed to the notion that new things must be better than old things because we are progressing and that implies that newer things will be superior to older things. Second, advertising often communicates the message that newer must be better.

On the other hand, when something "old" is painted in a positive light versus something "new," it is known as Appeal to Tradition. If the age of something is unrelated to the argument, than it is considered irrelevant. However, we must be careful because there are certain contexts in which age is absolutely relevant to the argument. If I say that my day-old gallon of milk is better than your three month old gallon of milk, I would not be committing the fallacy since the age of milk has a relevant and direct effect on it being drinkable.

EXAMPLE 1 (APPEAL TO NOVELTY):

"The Ten Commandments are outdated. How can a legal code written over 4,000 years ago be relevant in the 21st century? We need a new morality for a modern world.

ANALYSIS : The relevance of moral law should be evaluated based on the merits of each individual law and not on its age. What part of "thou shalt not kill" is outdated? What part of "thou shalt not steal" is outdated? What part of "thou shalt not covet thy neighbor's wife" is outdated? Obviously, the relevance of the commandments is independent of when they were written.

EXAMPLE 2 (APPEAL TO TRADITION):

"Our method of marketing has stood the test of time and has allowed us to stay in business for over fifty years. We don't need any of the new fancy methods of marketing. The old methods are simply better."

ANALYSIS : The usefulness or success of a marketing method should be evaluated independently of how old or new it may be. Because marketing attempts to appeal to a given culture at a given time, new methods are often very effective. For example, the internet has provided new opportunities for marketing that were not available 50 years ago. A strong case can even be made that businesses that do not update their marketing strategies will not be able to compete with those that do. Furthermore, an appeal to the "test of time" is also irrelevant for two reasons. First, history has shown us that erroneous ideas have often persisted for centuries. Second, just because something has worked for a long time, it does not follow that it will continue to work.

1.13 POISONING THE WELL:

This fallacy is a form of Ad Hominem and occurs when the opponent is attacked prior to making his case in an attempt to discredit anything he may later say. The person making the attack is attempting to bias the audience against his opponent. If an unfavorable claim about the opponent can be made (true or not) that discredits anything they have to say, then the issue itself does not have to be dealt with. It should be noted that presenting unfavorable attacks on the opponent is not evidence against the claims that they make.

EXAMPLE : Opening statement at a debate about God's existence: "My opponent in tonight's debate is an ignorant creationist "flat-earther", so you cannot believe a word he says. He is so ignorant, he will deny that he is a flat-earther, but every intelligent scientist knows that denying evolution is equivalent to believing the earth is flat. When you hear him deny what I have just said, you will know that he is not anintelligent scientist."

ANALYSIS : By poisoning any possible argument his opponent can make later, the presenter of the attack has attempted to bias the audience in his favor. Anything they hear from his opponent from this point forward will be tainted.

FALLACIES OF CLARITY

This category of fallacies includes arguments where lack of clarity leads to confusion and faulty reasoning. The lack of clarity can be introduced into an argument in numerous ways, but the results are typically the same—a lack of understanding of what exactly is being proposed.

2.1 EQUIVOCATION:

This fallacy occurs when a key term or terms in an argument are ambiguous. Usually a word or phrase in the argument appears with different meanings in different parts of the argument.

EXAMPLE : "The Gospels are considered God's word because the authors were inspired. Shakespeare was an inspired writer. Therefore, Shakespeare's writings should be considered God's word as well."

ANALYSIS : This argument fails because of the ambiguity of the word "inspired." In the case of the authors of the Gospels, the word "inspired" is used in the sense of a divine supernatural guidance. Regarding Shakespeare, the word inspired is used in the sense of an internal, completely natural intuitive impulse to write, similar to the inspiration of artists and musicians.

> THE LACK OF CLARITY CAN BE INTRODUCED INTO AN ARGUMENT IN NUMEROUS WAYS, BUT THE RESULTS ARE TYPICALLY THE SAME–A LACK OF UNDERSTANDING OF WHAT EXACTLY IS BEING PROPOSED.

2.2 ACCENT:

This fallacy occurs when the emphasis is placed on the wrong word or phrase. In other words, the accent or tone of voice changes the meaning of the statement.

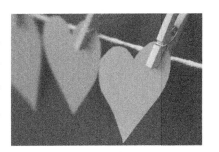

EXAMPLE : "I Love You."

ANALYSIS : This phrase can have four different meanings depending on which word is emphasized.

    I love you (as opposed to anyone else);

    I LOVE you (instead of like you);

    I love YOU (instead of someone else);

    I love you? (as in 'what makes you think that?').

This fallacy is common in written form because the "accent" cannot be heard when one reads. Many misunderstandings stem from misplacing the accent when one reads something.

2.3 AMPHIBOLE / AMBIGUITY:

This fallacy occurs when the grammatical structure of a statement is ambiguous. The words make sense but the meaning is obscure because of the grammatical construction. You cannot tell for sure how to relate the parts of the sentences.

EXAMPLE 1: "Save boxes and waste baskets."

ANALYSIS : This statement fails because the grammatical structure is ambiguous. It is impossible to determine if "waste" is being used as an adjective or a verb. Are we saving BOTH (boxes & waste baskets) or are we saving one (boxes) but wasting the others (baskets)?

EXAMPLE 2: "I live by the river; drop in some time.

ANALYSIS : Again, this statement fails because the grammatical structure is ambiguous. The object of the verb "drop" is uncertain. Does it mean drop in to see him at his home or drop into the river?

2.4 SIGNIFICANCE (CIRCUMSTANCE):

This fallacy occurs when specific circumstances or conditions alter the significance of the words or phrase.

EXAMPLE 1: "Enrique enjoyed killing 12 people with headshots."

ANALYSIS : This statement can be commendable or scandalous depending on the circumstances. It is one thing to speak of Enrique "killing 12 people with headshots" in a discussion of his favorite Xbox game. It is quite another to speak of Enrique "killing 12 people with headshots" when he is being interrogated by detectives investigating a school shooting.

Both the fallacies of Relevance and those of Clarity are common in everyday discourse. They can be found, quite abundantly, in newspaper articles and editorials, magazines, textbooks, etc. If the critical thinker is able to identify them, he can avoid the pitfalls of faulty reasoning.

INFORMAL LOGICAL FALLACIES PART 2

10

CHOCOLATE IS THE BEST FOOD BECAUSE I'VE NEVER TASTED ANYTHING BETTER.

I HAD A HEADACHE YESTERDAY, BUT BECAUSE I HAD CHOCOLATE FOR BREAKFAST, IT'S ALL GONE TODAY.

CHOCOLATE MADE ME FAT SO CHOCOLATE SHOULD BE MADE ILLEGAL.

CINDY LOOKED AT ME WHEN I BOUGHT MY CHOCOLATE. SHE MUST BE PLANNING TO STEAL IT.

FALLACIES OF PRESUMPTION

This category of fallacies includes arguments that make assumptions without sufficient support. These fallacies contain "hidden assumptions" that make the arguments invalid or unreasonable.

3.1 INAPPROPRIATE APPEAL TO AUTHORITY:

This fallacy occurs when an authority is cited in an attempt to add credence to a point being argued, but the authority cited is not an authority in the field relevant to the point being argued.

EXAMPLE : "Erwin Centrilli, Harvard Ph.D., agrees that my homemade lotion is excellent for treating all types of skin ailments. Thus you should buy my lotion."

ANALYSIS : This argument is fallacious because we are not given any hint regarding the area of specialty of the Ph.D. from Harvard. For all we know he could be a Ph. D. in Creative Writing or some other field that is totally irrelevant. It would only be a good argument if he was a Ph. D. in an area that specializes in treatments for skin ailments.

3.2 APPEAL TO IGNORANCE:

This fallacy occurs when someone attempts to persuade others to accept the conclusion of his argument as true simply on the basis that it has not been proven false, or conversely, that it is false simply because it has not been proven true. In other words, if the opponent cannot prove that the point of the argument is false, then it must be true and vice versa.

EXAMPLE 1 : "God does not exist because his existence has never been proven beyond a reasonable doubt."

ANALYSIS : This statement commits the fallacy because it assumes that if something's existence has not been proven beyond a reasonable doubt, it must not exist. Anything's existence is independent of its ever being proven or disproven.

EXAMPLE 2 : "God does exist because you cannot prove that He does not exist."

ANALYSIS : Although Christians often use this argument, the statement is also fallacious because it assumes that if something's inexistence has not been proven beyond a reasonable doubt, it must exist. It is the same type of faulty reasoning. Anything's existence is independent of its ever being proven or disproven. Not being able to prove God's inexistence is helpful in pointing out a major problem with atheism—atheism cannot be proven. However, it does not prove God's existence.

3.3 FALSE ALTERNATIVES/ BIFURCATION:

This fallacy occurs when the proponent establishes an argument based on a limited number of options, while leaving out at least one other possibility.

EXAMPLE : "There are only two types of people: those who rely on faith and those who rely on reason."

ANALYSIS : This is the type of argument that juxtaposes faith and reason as the only two alternatives to understanding reality. Usually the argument is presented to refute creationism (assumed to be based exclusively on faith) and promote evolution (assumed to be based exclusively on science). This argument is fallacious in part because it assumes that faith and reason are mutually exclusive with no other possible alternatives. However, it is the case that there is at least one other alternative as demonstrated by the undeniable existence of people who believe faith and reason go hand in hand. Thus it is not just possible, but evident, that faith and reason can coexist. The assumptions regarding each view are also false assumptions and thus invalidate the argument itself.

3.4 LOADED QUESTION:

This fallacy occurs when a question is poised in such a way as to trap the respondent into accepting the proposition. Regardless of how the respondent answers, the question forces an answer favorable to the proponent.

EXAMPLE : "Hey Victor, have you stopped beating your wife yet?"

ANALYSIS : In this loaded question, the assumption is already made that Victor beats his wife. If Victor does not beat his wife, how would he answer this question? A 'yes' would be affirming that he did beat his wife but has stopped. A 'no' would be affirming that he continues to beat his wife. The assumption that Victor beats his wife is not evidence that he does or does not. Furthermore, there is no room for the alternative of Victor not beating his wife.

3.5 QUESTIONABLE CAUSE:

This fallacy occurs when the proponent attempts to attribute a specific cause to an effect without strong evidence for the connection. Usually the effect can be the result of multiple causes, some of which are stronger than the proposed cause. This type of fallacy is rampant in the political arena as well as in the social battles fought on major issues such as abortion, marriage, etc.

EXAMPLE : "Obama won the 2008 election because he is African American and the African American community all voted for him."

ANALYSIS : This argument is a common example of questionable cause. While it is undeniable that president Obama is African American, how much of a role his ethnicity played in the election is very debatable. White people voted for him in large numbers, as did Hispanics. On the other hand, many African Americans voted for Romney. Furthermore, there are far more significant issues that voters considered when voting for him. Many believe those who voted for him did so primarily because they believed he would bring positive change to the nation and felt that he would better represent their interests. Regardless of where a voter stands on his election, this is not a good argument.

3.6 POST HOC FALLACY/ FALSE CAUSE:

This fallacy occurs when something is attributed to a cause simply because it follows it, assuming a faulty causal relationship. Just because one event follows another chronologically does not necessarily mean that one caused the other.

EXAMPLE 1 : "The day after Julie broke up with him, he had a nervous breakdown, so Christopher's parents are very upset at Julie for causing him to have the nervous breakdown."

ANALYSIS : This argument is guilty of the post hoc fallacy. Just because the nervous breakdown happened the day after the breakup, the arguer ignores other possible causes like other circumstances in Christopher's life during the months leading up to the breakdown. Or perhaps Julie's decision to breakup was the result of his already beginning to show signs of the nervous breakdown. It could even be argued that he was relieved to have finally gotten rid of Julie. Furthermore, the nervous breakdown could also have been caused by a chemical imbalance.

EXAMPLE 2 : "Eating five candy bars and drinking two sodas before a test helps me get better grades. I did that and got an A on my last test in history."

ANALYSIS : This argument is also guilty of the post hoc fallacy. This arguer ignores other possible causes like how much he had studied, how well he knew the material, or how easy the test was.

3.7 OVERSIMPLIFIED CAUSE FALLACY:

This fallacy occurs when an attempt is made to explain complex events or phenomena by attributing it to an oversimplified cause.

EXAMPLE : "Kids today spend too much time playing video games and as a result, most teenagers today don't enjoy reading. If we want kids to enjoy reading, we must severely restrict video game playing time."

ANALYSIS : While it may be true that some kids spend too much time playing video games, the disinterest in reading is more likely attributed to a host of causes including shortcomings in reading education, lack of or insufficient exposure to reading programs and materials, the explosion of online movies and entertainment, etc. Furthermore, restricting video game playing time may be beneficial for numerous reasons, but it doesn't follow that it will create a desire to read.

3.8 SWEEPING GENERALIZATION:

This fallacy occurs when generalizations are applied to cases where they don't apply. It is the fallacy of extending generalizations beyond their reach and ignoring exceptions.

EXAMPLE : "A large cup of coffee makes me clear, sharp, and energetic in the morning. Everyone should have a large cup of coffee in the morning to feel the same way."

ANALYSIS : Simply because the coffee has a specific effect on one person's metabolism, it does not follow that it will have the same effect on everyone's metabolism. In actuality, a large cup of coffee in the morning can be deadly to some people.

3.9 HASTY GENERALIZATION:

This fallacy occurs when a generalization is made without enough evidence or too few examples to support it. It is the fallacy of assuming that just because a few cases point in one direction, all cases will point in that direction as well.

EXAMPLE : "All four of my high school math teachers were very boring. Thus all math teachers are boring."

ANALYSIS : Four math teachers are not enough of a sampling to conclude that all math teachers everywhere are boring. There are millions of math teachers that the arguer has not been exposed to. Thus there may be many very interesting math teachers. The only thing that the arguer can safely conclude is that he found HIS (as opposed to ALL) math teachers were boring. It is also a matter of opinion, since some students may have found one or all of the same math teachers to be interesting. It may also be that he does not like math, and thus finds the subject itself boring.

3.10 SLIPPERY SLOPE:

This fallacy occurs when an attempt is made to persuade us that the acceptance or denial of the proposed position will lead to an avalanche of other actions that we don't necessarily desire. In other words, the decision will be the first step down a slippery slope and will result in a disastrous slide downhill. It is important to note that sometimes a decision may in fact lead us down a slippery slope and this is not a fallacy. What makes this a fallacy is the presentation of the resulting chain of events without showing the causal connection to the proposed position.

EXAMPLE : "Excessive video gaming is going to be the downfall of the United States. It starts with poor performance in school, leading to increased dropout rates. Thus the number of American kids entering college will dwindle leading to less qualified labor followed by a loss of competitive manufacturing which will destroy our economy. Dwindling numbers of college graduates will also put us farther behind in technology—making us vulnerable to being conquered by more technologically advanced countries. I hope they ban video gaming all together because I love the United States and I don't want to see us fall."

ANALYSIS : While excessive video gaming may be a problem in some circles, it cannot be connected directly as the cause of any of the events that are listed in slippery slope, and thus it is a fallacy to force the connection.

3.11 WEAK OR FALSE ANALOGY:

This fallacy occurs when a comparison/analogy between two things is presented to support an argument, but the things being compared aren't relevantly similar enough to justify the analogy. It is important to understand that analogies are not usually evaluated as good/bad or as right/wrong, but rather as strong or weak. The focus should be on relevant similarities, and thus the number of irrelevant differences or similarities is not a significant factor in evaluating the analogy.

EXAMPLE : Forrest Gump said, "My momma always said, 'Life is like a box of chocolates. You never know what you're gonna get.'"

ANALYSIS : While this is a memorable quote, it should be considered a very weak analogy, since there are no relevant similarities concerning the uncertainty of the future. Boxes of chocolates come with flavor guides in the box (eliminating all uncertainty), and you don't have to eat chocolates at all. Life is not relevantly similar to a box of chocolates.

3.12 INCONSISTENCY:

This fallacy occurs when two claims are made that are contradictory or inconsistent with each other and they both cannot be true at the same time and in the same sense.

EXAMPLE :

Carlos: *"Peter, what you are doing is wrong!"*

Peter: *"Why? What am I doing?"*

Carlos: *"You shouldn't tell those who disagree with you that they are wrong."*

Peter: *"Why?"*

Carlos: *"Because it is wrong to tell someone they are wrong."*

ANALYSIS : Carlos begins telling Peter he is wrong and then concludes by stating that it is wrong to tell someone he is wrong. Both statements are contradictory to each other, and thus they are inconsistent.

3.13 FALSE MODERATION:

This fallacy occurs when an argument is based on the assumption that the correct answer is always somewhere in the middle between extremes, and thus both sides are wrong. While the best answer may be somewhere in the middle, the answer must be justified independently of its "location" in the pendulum of possibilities.

EXAMPLE : "Abortionists claim that life begins at birth while the Pro- Lifers claim that life begins at conception. Thus the right answer is probably somewhere in the middle of these two extremes. Life probably begins 4½ months after conception."

ANALYSIS : When life begins is not predicated by when people think it does. Choosing an answer that is somewhere in the middle of the two extremes is completely random and fallacious.

3.14 NON SEQUITUR ("IT DOES NOT FOLLOW").

This fallacy occurs when a conclusion is drawn that does not follow from the given premises. The fallacy is to claim a relationship that is non-existent.

EXAMPLE : "Carlos refused to lend me the money I need to buy myself a car, and therefore Carlos must hate me."

ANALYSIS : It does not necessarily follow that Carlos hates him because he does not lend him the money. There could be any number of reasons for refusing him that have absolutely nothing to do with hate.

Fallacies of Presumption are as common as the other two categories. However, many of these fallacies are difficult to identify and require good hands-on knowledge and lots of practice. The rewards for such diligence are well worth it.

JESUS, THE MASTER OF CRITICAL THINKING

11

"Does not the ear test words, as the palate tastes its food?" *JOB 12:11*

It is easy to overlook Jesus the Thinker! Much has been written on Jesus the Redeemer, Jesus the Healer, Jesus the Miracle Worker, Jesus the Messiah, Jesus the Lord, etc., but the topic of Jesus as the greatest thinker of all time doesn't seem to get as much attention. Understanding Jesus, the Thinker, and his use of powerful arguments can prove to be invaluable in today's hostile world. The gospels dedicate an enormous amount of time and space describing how Jesus engaged the arguments and responded to the attacks that were launched against his truth claims. In doing so, Jesus engaged in a reasoned defense of the faith using critical thinking as one of his primary tools. As Douglas Groothuis so powerfully asserts, "When Jesus defended the crucial claims of Christianity—He was its founder, after all—He was engaging in apologetics, often with the best minds of first-century Judaism."[1] As Christians facing hostile arguments and attacks on our faith, there is much to learn from a closer look at some of those encounters.

PRELIMINARY CONSIDERATIONS

Jesus' engagements were undergirded by the desire to attract (not alienate) the lost. Beyond the strategies and specific critical thinking skills Jesus employed, we often find Jesus gently and respectfully seeking to persuade his opponents. He was not out to destroy them, but rather to enlighten them. Dallas Willard is on point when he affirms that, "Jesus' aim in utilizing logic is not to win battles, but to achieve understanding or insight in his hearers."[2] This ought to be our objective as well. We are called to demolish arguments—not people! We must constantly remind ourselves we are not trying to win arguments, but rather win people over to the truth of the Gospel.

Jesus' pedagogical strategy was very effective. He was able to engage his opponents in the thinking process by making them active participants instead of passive listeners. As Willard explains,

"...he does not try to make everything so explicit that the conclusion is forced down the throat of the hearer. Rather,

he presents matters in such a way that those who wish to know can find their way to, can come to, the appropriate conclusion as something they have discovered—whether or not it is something they particularly care for."[3]

As an educator I can attest to the effectiveness of this strategy. Too often we focus, almost exclusively, on presenting strong arguments and lists of evidences without really engaging the heart those we are attempting to persuade. Asking questions was one of Jesus' most successful strategies for getting his audience actively involved in what he was attempting to teach. These questions were meant to allow his opponents to reach certain conclusions on their own without him having to spell it out for them. We must learn the art of engaging people in thought and not just conversation.

Jesus was not concerned with being politically correct, especially when it came to unmasking errors in the opinions and arguments of his opponents. Whether he was speaking to the Pharisees or to a Roman governor, he was quick to correct fallacious thoughts and ideas. As Groothuis so clearly explains,

"Jesus engaged in extensive disputes, some quite heated, mostly with the Jewish intellectual leaders of His day. He did not hesitate to call into account popular opinion if it was wrong. He spoke often and passionately about the value of truth and the dangers of error, and He articulated arguments to support truth and oppose error." [4]

In an age of intolerance towards the Christian faith, we must continue to stand firmly for truth and against error. We must do this, as Jesus did, with the right attitude (gentleness and respect) and with strong sound arguments.

Jesus was a master logician. He used a wide variety of arguments and did so with extraordinary skill. An exhaustive review of Jesus' use of logic and critical thinking would be a very rewarding endeavor, but it is beyond the scope of this book. Nevertheless, let us consider five examples of Jesus employing various types of logical arguments.

1. JESUS' USE OF A FORTIORI ARGUMENTS

Jesus often used A Fortiori arguments. The Latin phrase 'a fortiori' means, "from something stronger." These are very persuasive arguments that build the case for a particular proposition by showing it has even stronger support than other related propositions commonly accepted as true. The structure is as follows:

PREMISE 1	Proposition "X" is widely accepted.
PREMISE 2	Support for proposition "Y" is even stronger than the support for proposition "X"
CONCLUSION:	Therefore, if proposition "X" is accepted, then proposition "Y" should be accepted all the more.

Consider the exchange found in Luke 13:14-16. Jesus was continually attacked for supposed violations of the Sabbath. In this passage, Jesus presents an A Fortiori argument in his defense as follows. I have put the arguments in standard form to make it easier to see exactly what Jesus was doing.

PREMISE 1	Loosening the cattle from their stall and taking them out to water on the Sabbath is widely practiced and accepted by the Pharisees.
PREMISE 2	This woman, a daughter of Abraham, (far more valuable than cattle) has been bound by Satan for 18 years and has also been loosed on the Sabbath.
CONCLUSION:	Therefore, if it is acceptable to loosen the cattle on the Sabbath, then it should be even more acceptable to loosen a daughter of Abraham.

2. JESUS' USE OF DISJUNCTIVE SYLLOGISMS (OR ARGUMENT BY ELIMINATION)

This type of argument, as we saw in Chapter 5, usually consists of a premise with two options, a second premise denying one of the options, and a conclusion asserting the remaining option. The idea is to eliminate all the options until only one is left, making it the only possible answer. The structure is as follows:

PREMISE 1	Either p or q
PREMISE 2	Not- q
CONCLUSION:	Therefore, p

Consider the words of Jesus in Luke 11:23. Here Jesus confronts the Pharisees with TWO Disjunctive Syllogism in the same verse as follows:

PREMISE 1	Either you are with me or you are against me.
PREMISE 2	They obviously were not with him (since they were attacking him)
CONCLUSION:	Therefore, they were against him.

PREMISE 1	Either you gather with me or you scattereth.
PREMISE 2	They obviously were not gathering with him
CONCLUSION:	Therefore, they were scattering.

3. JESUS' USE OF HYPOTHETICAL SYLLOGISMS (OR CHAIN ARGUMENT)

This type of argument, as we saw in Chapter 5, consists of three conditional statements linked together as follows:

PREMISE 1   If p then q

PREMISE 2   If q then r

CONCLUSION: Therefore, If p then r

Consider the words of Jesus to his disciples prior to sending them out in Matthew 11:40. He uses a Hypothetical Syllogism to explain the impact receiving their message would have on those who believed.

PREMISE 1   If they receive you, then they receive me.

PREMISE 2   If they receive me, then they receive him that sent me.

CONCLUSION: [implied] Therefore, If they receive you, then they receive him that sent me.

4. JESUS' USE OF SYLLOGISMS

A syllogism, as we saw in Chapter 5, is a three-line argument in which the premises lead to a definite conclusion. By using deductive reasoning, the argument establishes the conclusion without question. If the premises are true, then the conclusion must also be true. A common form is known as Modus Tollens and is structured as follows:

PREMISE 1	If p then q
PREMISE 2	Not- q
CONCLUSION:	Therefore, not p

Consider the words of Jesus in John 8:47 where he has been engaged in a long series of arguments with the Scribes and Pharisees that leads to this powerful argument.

PREMISE 1	If you are of God, then you heareth God's words
PREMISE 2	You hear them not
CONCLUSION:	Therefore, you are not of God

Sometimes the argument is easier to see in the paraphrase versions of the Bible. For example, this verse reads as follows in the Living Bible:

"Anyone whose Father is God listens gladly to the words of God. Since you don't, it proves you aren't his children."

5. JESUS WISDOM IN DEALING WITH THE HORNS OF A DILEMMA

The Pharisees were constantly trying to trap Jesus. They plotted and schemed to come up with arguments that would trap Jesus, regardless of his response. This is known in philosophy as a Dilemma or the fallacy of Bifurcation (Chapter 10). The argument presents two alternatives as if they were the only options and responding with either option gets you in trouble. That is why it is often referred to as being trapped in "the horns" of a dilemma. They tried this particular fallacy numerous times throughout Jesus' ministry, but were never successful. They were up against Jesus' mastery of logic and his divine wisdom.

Consider the passage in Matthew 22:15-22. Matthew prefaces the dialogue with the warning in verse 15 that the Pharisees "took counsel how they might entangle him in his talk" (KJV). They present Jesus with a dilemma regarding the paying of tributes (taxes) to Caesar. The two horns of the dilemma are presented in verse 17, "What thinkest thou? Is it lawful to give tribute unto Caesar, or not?" (KJV). If Jesus answered that it was lawful, then he was recognizing that Caesar was a higher authority than he was. If Jesus answered no, then he would be declaring himself an enemy of Caesar. However, they never anticipated Jesus' response. Jesus presented a third alternative—"Render therefore unto Caesar the things which are Caesar's; and unto God the things that are God's" (22:21 KJV). As was usually the case, "they marveled, and left him, and went their way" (22:22 KJV). Jesus' incredible wisdom was enough to leave anyone, even his most ardent opponents, speechless and in awe.

CONCLUSION

As we come to an end in this book, we must not lose sight of our God ordained responsibilities. We are called to always be prepared to give an answer to anyone that demands a reason for the hope that is within us, but how do we go about doing that? I think here, as in other areas of our walk, Jesus presents a wonderful model to follow. Jesus modeled for us the proper attitude to engage this world as well as the methodology. As Geisler and Zukeran suggest,

> **"Since reason and logical arguments were a part of Jesus's defense, the apologist and all Christians today should make this an area of study as they engage in the battle of ideas."[5]**

As we endeavor to engage in this dark world with the light of God's Truth, we must be careful not to skip the mind and focus only on the heart. God wants us to love Him with all of our hearts AND all of our minds. Only then will we be truly stable in our walk with the Lord. This should be paramount in our strategies for fulfilling our mission. Again, Geisler and Zukeran powerfully argue,

> **"The mission of transforming lives and bringing people to faith in Christ does not come by moving people emotionally; God does not bypass the mind to speak to the heart. Logic and well-reasoned arguments are required to refute false beliefs and turn people in the direction of truth."[6]**

Throughout many of the exercises that accompay each chapter, you are encouraged to find examples in the Bible. As we have seen above, spending time with Jesus, the Thinker, and studying his use of critical thinking, logic and powerful arguments can be very helpful in fulfilling our calling to engage the world with Truth.

Critical thinking is about learning how to think for yourself in a world that wants to tell you what to think. Mastering critical thinking will give you the tools you need to demolish bad arguments, develop good ones, defend your faith, and remove possible obstacles to faith in the minds of unbelievers.

NOTES

INTRODUCTION

[1] Gregory Bassham, William Irwin, Henry Nardone and James M. Wallace, Critical Thinking: A Student's Introduction, 3rd ed. (New York: McGraw-Hill, 2008), 1.

[2] However, due to the limited scope of this book, we will focus more on the first three areas and only indirectly on the fourth.

CHAPTER 1 THE PURSUIT OF TRUTH

[1] Ronald Nash. Life's Ultimate Questions: An Introduction to Philosophy,.(Grand Rapids: Zondervan, 1999), 228.

[2] See the section Tests of Truth later in the chapter for the methods of determining whether these statements are true or not.

[3] Nash, 228.

[4] Nash, 228-230.

[5] Nash, 229.

[6] An in-depth study of the word "truth" as it appears in both the Old and New Testaments is very profitable,

but lies outside the scope of this work.

[7] An outstanding breakdown of the biblical view of truth is found in Truth Decay by Douglas Groothuis, IVP, 2000. Especially helpful is chapter 3 titled, "The Biblical View of Truth" (pp.60-82) where the author provides and in-depth word study on "truth" as found in both the Old and New Testaments. He also presents and explains the 8 core aspects of biblical truth and their importance.

CHAPTER 2 CRITICAL THINKING PRINCIPLES

[1] Søren Kierkegaard, The Sickness Unto Death, trans. Howard V. Hong and Edna Hong (Princeton: Princeton University Press, 1980), 13.

[2] It must also be noted that several logical fallacies erroneously appeal to the majority in order to prove the accuracy of a statement or position. These will be addressed in chapters 9-10.

[3] See chapters 9-10 for a more in-depth consideration of this and other logical fallacies.

CHAPTER 3 OBSTACLES TO CRITICAL THINKING

[1] Nicholas Rescher, Objectivity: The Obligations of Impersonal Reason (Notre Dame: University of Notre Dame Press, 1997), 3-4; quoted in Thomas Howe, Objectivity in Biblical Interpretation (Tennessee: Advantage Books, 2004), 51-52. Examples and applications are added by the author of this book.

CHAPTER 4 CRITICAL THINKING AND PHILOSOPHY

[1] Different philosophers use different terminology for what we call the "category" of animals. Other common words include "group" or "class" and are basically synonymous when used to refer to the relationship between concepts.

[2] Encarta® World English Dictionary [North American Edition] © & (P) 1998-2007 Microsoft Corporation.

[3] See chapters 5-7 for further study of Logical Arguments.

CHAPTER 5 DEDUCTIVE ARGUMENTS GENERAL

[1] Geisler, Norman L. and Ronald M. Brooks. Come Let Us Reason: An Introduction to Logical Thinking (Grand Rapids: Baker Books, 1990.)

CHAPTER 7 INDUCTIVE ARGUMENTS

[1] These seven steps and their application to a specific argument are adapted from Gregory Bassham, William Irwin, Henry Nardone and James M. Wallace, Critical Thinking: A Student's Introduction, 3rd ed. (New York: McGraw-Hill, 2008), 316-318.

CHAPTER 11 CONCLUSION: JESUS, THE MASTER OF CRITICAL THINKING

[1] Douglas Groothuis. "Jesus: Philosopher and Apologist." http://www.equip.org/article/jesus-philosopher-and-apologist/ Accessed, 11/25/2015.

[2] Dallas Willard. "Jesus the Logician." Christian Scholar's Review, 1999, Vol. XXVIII, #4, 605-614.

[3] Ibid.

[4]Groothuis.

[5] Norman L. Geisler and Patrick Zukeran. The Apologetics of Jesus: A Caring Approach to Dealing with Doubters. (Grand Rapids: Baker Books, 2009) pg. 76.

[6] Ibid.

APPENDIX

APPENDIX
REVIEW EXERCISES

CHAPTER 1 THE PURSUIT OF TRUTH

KEY TERMS

- Truth
- Objective Truth
- Subjective Truth
- Test of Correspondence
- Test of Coherence
- Test of Pragmatism
- Relativism

THINK ABOUT IT...

1. Write 5 propositions that are objectively true.

2. Write 5 propositions that are objectively false.

3. Write 5 subjective propositions.

THINK A LITTLE HARDER...

4. Write a proposition that you can apply the Test of Correspondence to and it passes as Truth.

5. Write a proposition that you can apply the Test of Correspondence to and it proves to be false.

6. Write a proposition that you can apply the Test of Coherence to and it passes as Truth.

7. Write a proposition that you can apply the Test of Coherence to and it proves to be false.

8. Write a proposition that you can apply the Test of Pragmatism to and it passes as Truth.

9. Write a proposition that you can apply the Test of Pragmatism to and it proves to be false.

FOR THE GENIUSES...

10. List 3 lies the enemy uses to enslave humanity and provide the biblical truth that would set them free from those lies.

CHAPTER 2 CRITICAL THINKING PRINCIPLES

KEY TERMS

■ Logical Inconsistency

■ Practical Inconsistency

THINK ABOUT IT...

1. Write your own example dialogue that illustrates the importance of clarity in discourse (similar to the dialogue between Phil and Joe on page 37).

2. Write your own example dialogue that illustrates the importance of striving for accuracy (similar to the dialogue between Car Salesman and Naïve buyer on page 39).

3. Write your own example dialogue that illustrates the importance of pursuing precision (similar to the dialogue between Robbie and Joe on page 42).

4. Write an example of an argument that doesn't make logical sense and then analyze it (similar to the examples shown on page 44-45).

5. Write your own example of an irrelevant argument (similar to the four listed on pg.46-47).

THINK A LITTLE HARDER...

6. Write your own example of a logically inconsistent scenario (similar to Scenario 1, pg. 44).

7. Write your own example of a practically inconsistent scenario (similar to Scenario 2, pg. 46).

FOR THE GENIUSES...

8. How many of these principles can you find Jesus using in his
   dialogue with the Jewish authorities that were continually challenging
   him? List the principle and the passage where it is found.

CHAPTER 3 OBSTACLES TO CRITICAL THINKING

KEY TERMS

- Allegiance
- Conformity
- Personal Affinity
- Personal Bias
- Prejudice
- Wishful Thinking

THINK ABOUT IT...

1. Emotions have a way of clouding our judgment. Where is this explicitly taught in the Bible? Give references and a brief explanation.

2. Conformity is directly related to peer pressure. What does the Bible teach about conformity? Give reference and a brief explanation.

3. List three Proverbs that speak on the issue of associating with people who reject God's wisdom.

4. How does Acts 5:29 deal with the obstacle of ideological or political allegiances?

5. Personal biases have a tendency to adversely affect objectivity. What does the Bible teach regarding personal biases?
   Give reference and a brief explanation.

6. How does the Apostle Paul deal with "wishful thinking" and how it leads to false doctrines in 2 Timothy?
   List verses and a brief explanation.

THINK A LITTLE HARDER...

7. Provide a real-life example of the "Prejudices and Passions" obstacle to critical thinking.

8. Provide a real-life example of the "Conformity" obstacle to critical thinking.

9. Provide a real-life example of the "Personal Affinity" obstacle to critical thinking.

10. Provide a real-life example of the "Ideological or Political Allegiances" obstacle to critical thinking.

11. Provide a real-life example of the "Personal Bias" obstacle to critical thinking.

12. Provide a real-life example of the "Wishful Thinking" obstacle to critical thinking.

FOR THE GENIUSES...

13. Can you think of one or more additional obstacles to critical thinking not included in this chapter?

CHAPTER 4 CRITICAL THINKING AND PHILOSOPHY

KEY TERMS

- Causal Possibility
- Contradiction
- Counterexample
- Hypothesis
- Logical Possibility
- Necessary Condition
- Sufficient Condition
- Thought Experiment

THINK ABOUT IT...

1. Why is clarifying concepts important to the critical thinker?
2. Why is it important to come up with more than one hypothesis regarding any given question?
3. How do counter examples help in the process of testing hypotheses?
4. What do you consider the biggest challenge to properly implementing the 4th Step in the Philosophical Method?

THINK A LITTLE HARDER...

5. If someone says to you, "I don't believe in faith, I believe in science," how would you apply Step 1 of the Philosophical Method?
6. List three possible hypotheses for the following question: "What is the relationship between faith and science?"
7. Can you eliminate any of the three possible hypotheses listed above by providing a counterexample? (Note: A contrary biblical passage is also considered a counter example or counter argument).

8. Apply Step 4 to the question of faith and science. Provide what you think is the best answer/hypothesis and explain why.

SKILL DRILLS

Necessary & Sufficient Conditions

Answer the following with T/F.

1. Being stupid is a necessary condition for flunking out of college.

2. Getting only "F's" is a sufficient condition for flunking out of college.

3. Believing in God is a necessary condition for being a Christian.

4. Being born in Texas is a sufficient condition for being an American.

5. Being omnipotent is a necessary condition for being God.

6. Being rich is a sufficient condition for being happy.

Logical & Causal Possibility

Answer the following questions with T/F.

7. It is causally possible that an earthquake will destroy all buildings in New York next week.

8. It is logically possible for Joe Biden to turn into a frog.

9. It is causally impossible that one person robs all the banks in Boston during one day.

10. Being causally possible is a necessary condition for being logically possible.

11. Being causally possible is a sufficient condition for being logically possible.

Thought Experiments and Counterexamples

Refute the following hypotheses by finding logically possible scenarios that constitute counterexamples to the claims.

12. In order to be completely happy it is necessary to have shelter and some clothing.

13. It is a necessary condition for being a person to be capable of self-motivated activities.

14. No rational person would choose to have an abortion if she knew that a fetus has a soul right from the time of conception.

15. Every person pursues those things that bring her pleasure.

16. All people who commit suicide are unhappy and depressed.

FOR THE GENIUSES…

17. Apply the Philosophical Method (pp. 60) to the following philosophical question. "Why is there something rather than nothing?"

CHAPTER 5 DEDUCTIVE ARGUMENTS GENERAL

KEY TERMS

- Antecedent
- Argument
- Conclusion
- Consequent
- Deductive argument
- Disjunctive syllogism
- Hypothetical syllogism
- Invalid

- Logic
- Modus ponens
- Modus tollens
- Premises
- Sound argument
- Syllogism
- Valid

THINK ABOUT IT...

1. List five things that you know about the opposite gender (boys or girls).

2. List two premises for each of the above truths. Begin with one of the words on pg. 76.

3. Why is it important for an argument to be valid?

4. Why is it important for an argument to be sound?

5. Write your own example of a valid argument that IS NOT sound.

THINK A LITTLE HARDER...

6. Come up with three original Modus Ponens arguments and write them in standard form.

7. Come up with three original Modus Tollens arguments and write them in standard form.

8. Come up with three original Disjunctive Syllogisms and write them in standard form.

9. Come up with three original Hypothetical Syllogisms and write them in standard form.

Developing supporting premises

Construct some arguments that provide support for the following conclusions. You don't have to agree with the conclusion; this is simply an exercise in logic.

10. The Bible is God's Word to mankind.

11. Everyone should do what make them happiest.

12. Angels exist.

13. Dr. Pepper is the best soft drink available today.

14. God is good.

15. Politicians have to lie to be successful.

16. Men are superior to women.

17. Tupac is still alive.

18. Aliens are planning to invade Earth.

Arguments in Standard Form

Put the following arguments into standard form:

19. Telemarketers call my phone hundreds of times a day. Telemarketers are annoying to me. I find it very annoying to have to the phone ringing constantly.

20. Elevators are scary. One time my friend Chris got stuck in an elevator for 7 hours. It is scary to be stuck in a such a small area for so long.

21. To be a millionaire you have to be lucky or born into wealth. I will never be a millionaire since I am not very lucky nor was I born into a wealthy family.

22. Someone told me that you are planning to spend 24 hours playing on your X-Box this weekend. I think that is morally wrong.

Everyone knows that we must invest our time in things that make a difference in the lives of others. Spending the 24 hours volunteering at a homeless shelter would make a much bigger difference in the lives of others than playing X-Box.

Implied Premises

Put the following arguments into standard form
and add the premise that is implied but not stated explicitly:

23. Victoria is not going to be successful in life. She has no desire to succeed.

24. Either we go to work or we go fishing tomorrow. Therefore, I'm going fishing tomorrow.

25. Garbage collectors make over $40,000 per year without having attended college. Thus, it is a waste of time to attend college.

26. Demi is not good at playing soccer. The coach said you have to be athletic to be good at playing soccer.

27. Cathy is very happy with her marriage to Bert. Everyone knows Christian men make great husbands.

FOR THE GENIUSES...

28. Find a Biblical passage in which we can see a clear example of a logical argument that could be expressed in premises and conclusion.

CHAPTER 6 DEDUCTIVE ARGUMENTS: CATEGORICAL SYLLOGISMS

KEY TERMS

- Affirmative Copula
- Categorical Proposition
- Categorical Syllogism
- Copula
- Distribution of Terms
- Equivocation
- Major Premise
- Major Term
- Middle Term
- Minor Premise
- Minor Term
- Negative Copula

- Particular Quantifiers
- Predicate Term
- Quality
- Quantifiers
- Quantity
- Subject Term
- Type A proposition
- Type E proposition
- Type I proposition
- Type O proposition
- Universal Quantifies

THINK ABOUT IT...

1. Find three categorical statements in magazine or newspaper editorials and identify the type.

2. Find one of each type of categorical statement in the Bible.

THINK A LITTLE HARDER...

3. Come up with three original Categorical Syllogisms and write them in standard form (P1/P2/Conc).

SKILL DRILLS

Distribution of terms

Identify these statements as Type A, E, I, or O. Then determine if the term in italics is distributed or undistributed.

4. All birds have feathers.

5. Some doctors are not cardiologists.

6. Some stores are expensive.

7. No one is reliable.

8. Dogs bark at strangers.

9. Everyone was left in the dark.

10. Some people can be very difficult.

11. Carpenters are not very detail oriented.

12. Some cardiologists don't care about their patients.

13. The Bible is true.

Identifying Deductive Arguments (Chapters 4 & 5)

Put the following deductive arguments into standard form and determine whether the arguments are in the form of modus ponens, modus tollens, disjunctive syllogism, hypothetical syllogism or categorical syllogism.

14. Either the tooth fairy exists or my parents have been lying to me. The tooth fairy does not exist. I know therefore that my parents have been lying to me.

15. If God exists then life has meaning and purpose. Therefore, life has meaning and purpose since God exists.

16. If I go to Orlando, I will visit Islands of Adventure. If I visit Islands of Adventure, I will have fun. Therefore, if I go to Orlando, I will have fun.

17. All athletes are jocks. All jocks are dumb. Thus all athletes are dumb.

18. If you drink plenty of fluids you won't dehydrate. You are dehydrated. Therefore you have not had plenty of fluids.

FOR THE GENIUSES...

19. Find an example of a categorical argument in the Bible and put it in standard form.

CHAPTER 7 INDUCTIVE ARGUMENTS

KEY TERMS

- Abductive argument
- Analogical argument
- Enumerative inductive argument
- Inductive argument
- Ockham's Razor
- The Principle of Conservatism

THINK ABOUT IT...

1. What makes an inductive argument strong?

2. What makes an inductive argument weak?

THINK A LITTLE HARDER...

3. Come up with three original Enumerative Inductive Arguments and write them in standard form.

4. Come up with three original Analogical Arguments and write them in standard form (one in each format).

5. Come up with three original Abductive Arguments and write them in standard form.

6. Give an example where Ockham's Razor is not effective.

7. Give an example where the Principle of Conservatism is not effective

SKILL DRILLS

Evaluating "best explanations"

Discuss under what situations the following "best explanations" would seem unreasonable. Where possible, make use of the principle of Ockham's Razor and the Principle of Conservatism.

8. The best explanation for why I failed freshman English is that I simply don't like the teacher.

9. The best explanation for why some people are rich and others are poor is that the rich people are hardworking and the poor people are lazy.

10. The best explanation for why so many people drink alcohol is that alcohol is very inexpensive.

11. The best explanation for why the Bible cannot be true is that it was written by people.

12. The best explanation for why I am fat is that we live in a country with too much food.

Evaluating "best explanations"

13. Bananas are yellow. Yellow things are beautiful. Therefore, bananas are beautiful.

14. Blind people wear dark glasses. Jonathan is wearing dark glasses. It follows therefore that Jonathan is blind.

15. I have never seen a red mustang with white zebra stripes. Thus such a car does not exist.

16. You have to be very dumb to fail a spelling test. Carlos got a 48 on his spelling test. It follows therefore that Carlos is very dumb.

17. Everyone decides for themselves what is right and what is wrong. Being able to decide such matters is a sign of being truly free. Therefore, everyone is truly free.

FOR THE GENIUSES...

18. Find an example of each type of inductive argument in the Bible (Abductive Argument, Analogical Argument, Enumerative Inductive Argument

CHAPTER 8 FORMAL LOGICAL FALLACIES

KEY TERMS

■ Fallacy

■ Formal Fallacy

■ Informal Fallacy

THINK ABOUT IT...

1. Why is it important to know the fallacies?

2. What do the fallacies of Illicit Major, Illicit Minor, and Illicit Middle have in common?

3. What makes it difficult to identify the Four Term fallacy?

THINK A LITTLE HARDER...

4. Give your own unique example of the Illicit Major fallacy.

5. Give your own unique example of the Illicit Minor fallacy.

6. Give your own unique example of the Illicit Middle fallacy.

7. Give your own unique example of the Four Term fallacy.

8. Give your own unique example of the Denying the Antecedent fallacy.

9. Give your own unique example of the Affirming the Consequent fallacy.

FOR THE GENIUSES...

10. Can you find an example of a Formal Fallacy in a magazine or newspaper editorial article? It may require you to put arguments in standard form first and then evaluate.

CHAPTER 9 INFORMAL LOGICAL FALLACIES (1)

KEY TERMS

▌ Clarity

▌ Relevance

THINK ABOUT IT...

1. Find a fallacious editorial article in the newspaper and list all fallacies of relevance and clarity you find in the piece.

2. Find examples of fallacies in a political speech.

THINK A LITTLE HARDER...

3. Come up with your own example of an Ad Hominem Abusive fallacy.

4. Come up with your own example of a Tu Quoque fallacy.

5. Come up with your own example of a Mob Appeal fallacy.

6. Come up with your own example of a Chronological Snobbery fallacy.

7. Come up with your own example of a Poisoning the Well fallacy.

8. Come up with your own example of an Equivocation fallacy.

9. Come up with your own example of an Accent fallacy.

10. Come up with your own example of an Amphibole fallacy.

11. Come up with your own example of a Significance fallacy.

SKILL DRILLS

Fallacies of Relevance

Complete the following matching exercise.

a. Ad Hominem Abusive

b. Ad Hominem Circumstantial

c. Tu Quoque

d. Appeal to Fear

e. Appeal to Force

f. Mob Appeal

g. Snob Appeal

h. Appeal to Pity

i. Straw Man

j. Red Herring

k. Begging the Question

l. Chronological Snobbery

m. Poisoning the Well

12. This is a "look who's talking" claim.

13. This is an attempt to persuade by force.

14. Trying to prove a conclusion by including it in a premise.

15. Appealing to the "common man" emotion.

16. Attempting to persuade someone by appealing to elitism.

17. A strong personal attack to avoid the issue at hand.

18. When someone misrepresents the opposing view in a manner easy to destroy.

19. Appealing to the age of something as a basis for acceptance or rejection of it

20. Attacking the reputation of the opponent prior to his presenting his argument.

21. Attempting to win an argument by scaring the opponent with possible consequences.

22. Using an irrelevant joke, story, or issue to change the subject of the debate

23. Attempting to persuade someone by making them feel sorry about someone.

24. A strong attack of the circumstances to avoid dealing with the real issues.

Read these fallacies of relevance and identify which specific fallacy is shown.

25. Don't vote for Peter because he is a stupid, foot-licking dung farmer.

26. Most people are satisfied with ordinary pens, but at Mont Blanc we manufacture an elite pen for those who demand the highest level of excellence in writing instruments.

27. Christians are opposed to science and public schools. Such ignorance disqualifies them as good parents and makes anything they say irrelevant. We shouldn't believe anyone who denies the advances of science or fails to see the value of public education.

28. Do you want the nation plunged into war? Vote for McQuilkin.

29. Museum Guide: "This fossil is 150 million years old."

Cathy: "How do you know they are so old?"

Museum Guide: "Because of the stratus they were found in."

Cathy: "How do you know the date of that stratus?"

Museum Guide: "Because of the fossils we find in that stratus."

30. Why should I get in trouble for talking, when everyone else was talking too?

31. You should hire me because I really need this job. I have eleven hungry children, and my husband died two years ago.

FALLACIES OF CLARITY

Complete the following matching exercise.

a. Equivocation

b. Accent

c. Amphibole

d. Significance

32. When emphasis is place on wrong word or phrase.

33. When grammatical structure of a statement is ambiguous.

34. When key terms in an argument are ambiguous.

35. When specific circumstance change the meaning of terms.

Read these fallacies of relevance and identify which specific fallacy is shown.

36. She told me this hat looked good on me. I can't believe she would imply that the other hats don't look good on me.

37. The Pastor will be talking about sex in church.

38. Smoking weed is illegal. Therefore, I cannot smoke the weeds I remove from my garden.

39. I once shot an elephant in pajamas.

40. Ricardo told the poker dealer to hit him.

41. Cell phone communication is a miracle of modern science, so how can anyone say that miracles don't happen in our times?

42. Find an example of a Fallacy of Relevance or Clarity being used by the Jewish authorities in their arguments with Jesus.

CHAPTER 10 INFORMAL LOGICAL FALLACIES (2)

KEY TERMS

▪ Presumption

THINK ABOUT IT...

1. Find an example of a Fallacy of Presumption in advertising (could be from television commercial or from written advertising found in newspapers and magazines).

THINK A LITTLE HARDER...

2. Come up with your own example of an Appeal to Ignorance Fallacy.

3. Come up with your own example of a Questionable Cause Fallacy.

4. Come up with your own example of a Sweeping Generalization Fallacy.

5. Come up with your own example of a Hasty Generalization Fallacy.

6. Come up with your own example of an Inconsistency Fallacy.

7. Come up with your own example of a Non-Sequitur Fallacy.

SKILL DRILLS

Fallacies of Presumption

Complete the following matching exercise.

a. Appeal to Authority	h. Sweeping Generalizations
b. Appeal to Ignorance	i. Hasty Generalizations
c. False Alternatives/Bifurcation	j. Slippery Slope
d. Question	k. Weak or False Analogy
e. Questionable Cause	l. Inconsistency
f. Post Hoc/False Cause	m. False Moderation
g. Oversimplified Cause	n. Non-Sequitur

Definitions

1. When all of the options are not considered in an argument.

2. Comparing two things that are not relevantly similar.

3. When generalizations are made without sufficient evidence.

4. When generalizations are applied to cases where they don't apply.

5. Defaulting to the "middle" position as the best choice.

6. Relying on contradictory claims to make a point.

7. When an "expert" in an irrelevant field is used to support a claim.

8. When an inquiry is meant to trap the respondent.

9. Drawing a conclusion from premises that don't follow.

10. When something is assumed to be true because it has not been proven false.

11. Using a series of possible but baseless outcomes to persuade acceptance or denial of a claim.

12. When a cause that is too simple is attributed to an effect that is too complex.

13. When a cause is attributed to an effect simply because it occurred prior to the event.

14. When a cause is attributed to an effect without a clear connection.

Read these fallacies of relevance and identify which specific

fallacy is shown.

15. There are two types of people in the world: those who own a BMW and those who wish they did.

16. My gardener, who holds a Ph. D. in Grass Cutting, told me Einstein's theory of relativity is a bunch of bologna. I guess Einstein wasn't that smart after all.

17. My wife is like a car without brakes. Once she starts fussing there is no way to stop her.

18. I wanted to stop at Starbucks this morning but I decided not to. Spending so much on coffee could lead me to waste my savings and become indebted. Then if I lose my job, I won't have any funds to live on, and I will lose my house and my car. I'm glad I didn't stop at Starbucks, I'm not willing to lose everything for a cup of coffee.

19. Ever since I ate popcorn on Sunday, my insomnia is gone, and I sleep like a baby. Popcorn cured my insomnia.

20. No one has been able to prove that aliens don't exist. Therefore, there must be aliens somewhere out there.

FOR THE GENIUSES...

21. Find an example of a Fallacy of Presumption that was used against Jesus in the Gospels and which he refuted in his response.

Made in the USA
Monee, IL
21 August 2021